BOOK

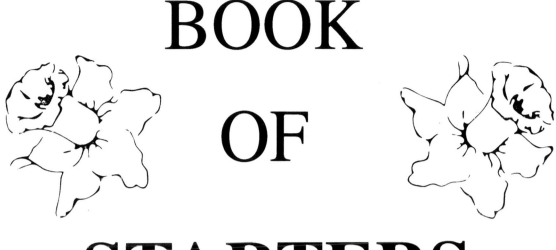

OF

STARTERS

This book was collated and edited by
Belinda Pinckney

My thanks go to Mr Derek Mowatt
Principal Teacher of Art
at The Academy School, Perth
under whose guidance his students have produced
these absolutely stunning drawings

MARIE CURIE CANCER CARE
PERTHSHIRE

Printed by Danscot Print Ltd
6-8 Kinnoull Street, Perth
Scotland

Marie Curie Cancer Care
Charity Reg No 207994   ISBN No 0-9516454-2-0

Following on 1993's Perthshire Pudding Party, on April 29th, 1994, we staged the Perthshire Starter Party, held in conjunction with the Perth Food Festival, in The City Hall, Perth. And following on the highly successful Book of Puddings we are printing this Book of Starters, with some of the recipes, chosen by the judges, to be representative of a diverse selection of the best starters.

My grateful thanks go to our four judges who generously devoted a great deal of their time to judging this event. They are all good friends to Marie Curie Cancer Care and it is very largely due to them that this event went off so successfully.

The judges were:

Mary Rose Reville
winner of The Pudding Party

Katie Targett-Adams
Scottish Junior Master Chef 1994

David Wilson
The Peat Inn, Fife

John Webber
Kinnaird House Hotel

The Peat Inn
is one of Scotland's most celebrated restaurants. It is situated
in the tiny village of the same name just six miles from
St. Andrews in the East Neuk of Fife. The cooking reflects the
wonderful produce of Scotland and the pleasures of the table
can be extended by an overnight stay in one of the luxury
suites in The Residence.

Kinnaird
is a private country house which is now open to the public as a
hotel. It is surrounded by a beautiful estate of 9,000 acres
with breath-taking views of the moors and the Tay Valley.
The kitchen has already established itself for fine cuisine
and is open for lunch and dinner seven days a week from
March to January.

CONTENTS

Goat Cheese Galette   1
Emma Scott

Salmon Mousse   2
Helen Gordon

Fresh Asparagus Mousse   5
Caroline Stroyan

Mattjes Herring Salad   6
Ray Kuhn

Chicken Liver Pate   6
Martha Spencer

Roasted Italian Peppers   7
Jane O'Dell

Cucumber and Cheese Mousse   8
Lady Sarah Walter

Trout Mousse   9
Silla Keyser

Filo Pastry Flan with Courgette & Tomato   1 0
John Webber

Smoked Fish Mousse   1 1
Mrs Lily Gibb

Marinated Kippers   1 2
Smoked Haddock Pate   1 2
The Patients of Macmillan House

Garlic Mushrooms   1 2
Ray Kuhn

Mushroom Tarts   1 3
C. Watt

Scallop & Salmon Ceviche   1 4
Ursula Mackenzie

Watercress Roulade   1 4
Mrs Katherine Duff

Fish Saute with Hazelnut Topping   1 5
Katie Targett-Adams

Crostini   1 6
Angela Straker

Strathtay Savoury Tartlets   1 6
Annie Fraser

Game & Herb Sausage Terrine   17
    The Salutation Hotel

Italian Cabbage Parcels   18
    Thorntons Ws, Solicitors

Creams of Chicken with Tarragon & Pink Grapefruit   19
    Elizabeth Glenn

Mushroom Brioches   20
    Janet Scott

Avocado & Prawn Cheese Puffs   21
    Caroline Stroyan

Prawn & Cream Cheese Pate   22
    Jean McIntyre

Haggis Stillaig   22
    Hazel Barber

Hunter's Pate   22
    Mrs. F. Hunter

Harlequin Mousse   23
    Roe Cassels

Sole Terrine with Fresh Herbs   24
    David Wilson

Parcels of Gigha Goat's Cheese   26
    Richard Lyth

Smoked Cod's Roe Mousse   27
    The Hon. Mrs. F.G. Gillies

Salmon Mould   27
    Mrs Jean McCormack

Avocado Mousse with Sun-Dried Tomatoes   28
    The Hon. Mrs. Ranald Noel-Paton

Anchovy Pate   28
    Lady Montgomery

Sole & Salmon Rolls   29
    Kate Leathley

Hot & Sour Pickled Prawns   29
    Kathleen Blythe

Mousseline of Sole with Prawns   30
    Peggy Thomson

Spicy Vegetables in Crispy Baskets   32
    Mrs Andrea Targett-Adams

Neopolitan Savoury Mousse   33
    Mrs James Barr

Pears & Stilton   3 4
Mrs Bruce Hamilton

Steamed Asparagus Rolled in Salmon   3 6
John Webber

Hot Mushroom and Onion Sandwich   3 7
Katie Targett-Adams

Fish, Spinach & Watercress Terrine   3 8
Morag Henderson

Tricolor d'Ecosse   3 8
Meriel Hoare

Funghi al Chianti   3 9
The Governor, Friarton Prison

Potted Prawn Pate   3 9
Grizel Stewart

Julienne of Pigeon Breats   4 0
David Wilson

Blue Cheese & Pear Tartlets   4 1
Mary Rose Reville

Summer Seas Roulade   4 2
Kenneth Nicol

Cream Cheese Stuffed Avocadoes   4 3
Gail Barclay

Stuffed Tomatoes or Avocados   4 4
Mrs. M.H. Gow

Vegetable Starter   4 4
Mrs Timothy Holcroft

Leek, Haddock & Herb Mousses   4 5
Danscot

Cod & Crab Cakes   4 6
John Webber

Smoked Salmon Star   4 8
Katie Targett-Adams

Tomato & Horseradish Creamy Jelly   5 1
Lady Macdonald

Walnut & Spring Onion Tarts   5 2
Barbara Mackenzie

Mushrooms In Port   5 3
Julian Perera

Layered Fish Mousse   5 4
Lady Montgomery

Melon with Elderberry   5 4
Kate Leathley

Quail's Egg & Walnut Salad   5 5
Judy Nicol

Smoked Salmon Tartlets   5 6
Mrs. C. Dunbar

Hot Smoked Trout   5 7
Belinda Pinckney

Creamy Chicken Mousse   5 8
Mrs Janice Shepherd

Melon Balls, Shrimps & Cucumber   5 9
Mrs Ann Wimberley

Pasta Prawn Cocktail   6 0
Norma Butcher

Khura Cream   6 0
Leonie Nichol

Baked Camembert with Gooseberry Sauce   6 2
Mary Rose Reville

Hummus   6 3
Dee Cameron

Caviar Pie   6 4
Sara Jane Gilbey

A Gateau of Smoked Trout   6 5
Mrs R Caffrey

Sally's Egg Mousse   6 5
Belinda Pinckney

Tuna Moulds   6 7
Mrs Marion B Hazel

Cheese & Celery Hot Pots   6 7
Mrs Gray

Mushroom Starter   6 9
Mrs David Noble

Mushroom Almond Terrine   6 9
Margaret Brown

Piroshki   7 0
Gordon Sangster

Smoked Trout Pate   **7 0**
June Lawson

Cheese Creams   **7 1**
Mrs. C. Moncrieff

Chicken Liver & Peanut Pate **7 1**
A. Hart

Chicken Liver Parfait   **7 2**
Patsy Walker

Prawn Pate   **7 3**
Mrs David Anstice

Tuna & Orange Pate   **7 3**
Mrs Thom

Fruity Cheese Cocktail   **7 3**
Martha Noel-Paton

Carrot Mousse with Prawn Sauce **7 4**
Idonea Crossley

Smoked Chicken with Tomato & Ginger **7 5**
Fiona Bird

Smoked Mackeral Suedoise   **7 6**
Fifi Scott

SOUPS

Curried   Parsnip   Soup   3
   Mrs. H. Wilson

Iced   Rhubarb   Soup   3
   Mrs. Henry Illingworth

Watercress   Soup   4
   Stuart Lackie

Cauliflower,Smoked   Cheese   &   Mustard   Soup   3 0
   Fiona Goldthorpe

Potage   Solferino   3 1
   The Red Cross

Chilled   Melon   Soup   4 3
   Mrs Alison McLeod

Courgette   &   Mint   Soup   4 7
   Lorna Muir

Carrot   &   Orange   Soup   4 7
   Brian J. Mackie

Potage   de   Poisson   Fume   4 9
   Mr. T.J.W. Ross

Rooti   Tutti   Soup   5 0

Red   Pepper   Soup   5 0
   Mrs Ian Petrie

Shrimp   &   Sour   Cream   Soup   6 1
   Mrs. R. Stormonth-Darling

Italian   Tomato   Soup   6 1
   The Manna House

Vichysoisse   6 4
   The Hon. Mrs. F.G. Gillies

Cold   Tomato   Soup   6 6
   Tim Holcroft

Apple   &   Cashew   Nut   Soup   6 6
   Mrs. D. Radin

Cauliflower   &   Stilton   Soup   6 8
   Mrs Charles Watt

Senglese   Soup   6 8
   Margaret Mills

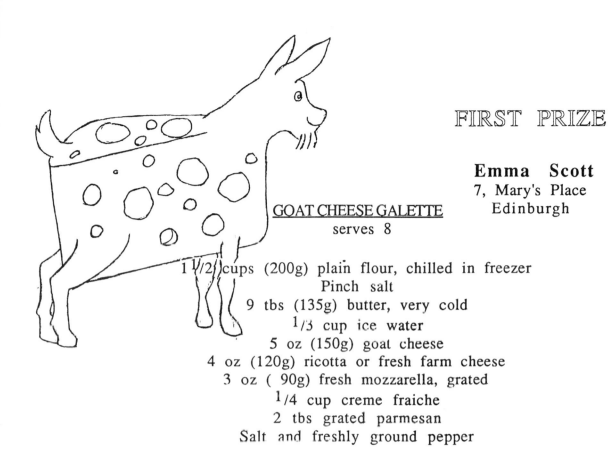

Emma   Scott
7, Mary's Place
Edinburgh

GOAT CHEESE GALETTE
serves 8

1 1/2 cups (200g) plain flour, chilled in freezer
Pinch salt
9 tbs (135g) butter, very cold
1/3 cup ice water
5 oz (150g) goat cheese
4 oz (120g) ricotta or fresh farm cheese
3 oz (90g) fresh mozzarella, grated
1/4 cup creme fraiche
2 tbs grated parmesan
Salt and freshly ground pepper

Place the flour and salt on a cold work surface.   Cut the butter
into 1/2" (12mm) pieces.   With a pastry scraper, cut the butter
into the flour & salt until roughly the size of peas (but no
smaller).   Add all of the water and mix until it forms a ball.
Alternately this pastry can be made in the electric mixer using
the same technique.   Roll the dough on a well floured surface
into a 15" (40cm) circle.   Place in the refrigerator while you
assemble the filling.

Mix together the goat cheese, ricotta, mozzarella, creme fraiche
and parmesan.   Mix well and season with salt and pepper.

Remove the pastry from the refrigerator.   Spread the cheese
over the pastry leaving a 2 1/2" (6cm) border uncovered.   Fold
the uncovered edge of the pastry over the cheese, pleating it to
make it fit.

Bake at 350F (180C) for 35 to 40 minutes until golden brown.
Slide the galette off the pan and onto a cooling tray.   Leave for
5 minutes, then serve with olive oil, prepared as follows: add
olives, fresh rosemary & oregano, and a clove or garlic to olive
oil.   Warm and leave to infuse.

SALMON MOUSSE
serves 12 people

Make 1 pint aspic and cool.

Mix together:
4 tsp grated onion
1 tsp anchovy essence
10 tbsp thick mayonnaise
2 tbsp tomato sauce
1 tbsp vinegar
4 tbsp lemon juice
1 tbsp sugar
6 tbsp chopped gherkins
10 drops tabasco
Season to taste.

Add aspic to the above ingredients plus
$1^1/2$ lbs cooked flaked salmon.

Add $3/4$ pint stiffly whipped cream.

Mix well and serve with sauce vert:
i.e. mayonnaise with a mixture of parsley, chives, tarragon and spinach.

Helen Gordon
Lude
Blair Atholl

WINNING SOUPS

Mrs. A. Wilson
Oakbank
Auchterarder

CURRIED PARSNIP SOUP

1 1/2 oz margarine	2 lb parsnips, peeled & sliced
1 onion, skinned and chopped	1 potato, peeled & sliced
1 tsp curry powder	1/2 tsp ground cumin
2 pt chicken stock	salt & pepper
3 oz single cream	10 fl oz milk

1. Melt margarine, add parsnip, onion & potato. Saute for 3 minutes.
2. Stir in curry powder & cumin. Cook for 2 minutes.
3. Add stock, bring to boil and simmer until vegetables are tender.
4. Puree in blender until smooth.
5. Reheat, adjust seasoning, add cream and milk.

Villa Rose
Archiestown
by Aberlour

ICED RHUBARD SOUP

1 lb fresh rhubarb and a slice of
        lemon.
Tip into boiling water to cover.
 Add:
1 heaped dessertspoon
        finely grated ginger.
2 tablespoons brown sugar.
Bring back to boil and simmer until
        just cooked.
Strain off liquid.
Add dessertspoonful
        preserved ginger juice.
Cool.
Add wine glass whisky.

Mrs Henry Illingworth

3

JUNIOR WINNER

Stuart Lackie
St Columba's High School
Perth

WATERCRESS SOUP

$1/2$ large onion
1 large floury potato
12.5g butter
$1 1/2$ bunches of watercress
$1/2$ litre chicken stock
salt & pepper
60ml double cream

Peel and finely chop onion. Peel and chop or grate potatoes. Melt butter in a saucepan, add onions and potatoes and turn till coated in butter. Cover and cook gently for 10 minutes.

Wash, dry and chop watercress leaves and stalks, reserving some whole leaves. Add to pan with stock and bring to the boil. Cover and simmer for 15 minutes.

Rub soup through sieve or puree in blender. Return to pan, add reserved watercress leaves and reheat. Taste and adjust seasoning. Serve hot or cold with cream.

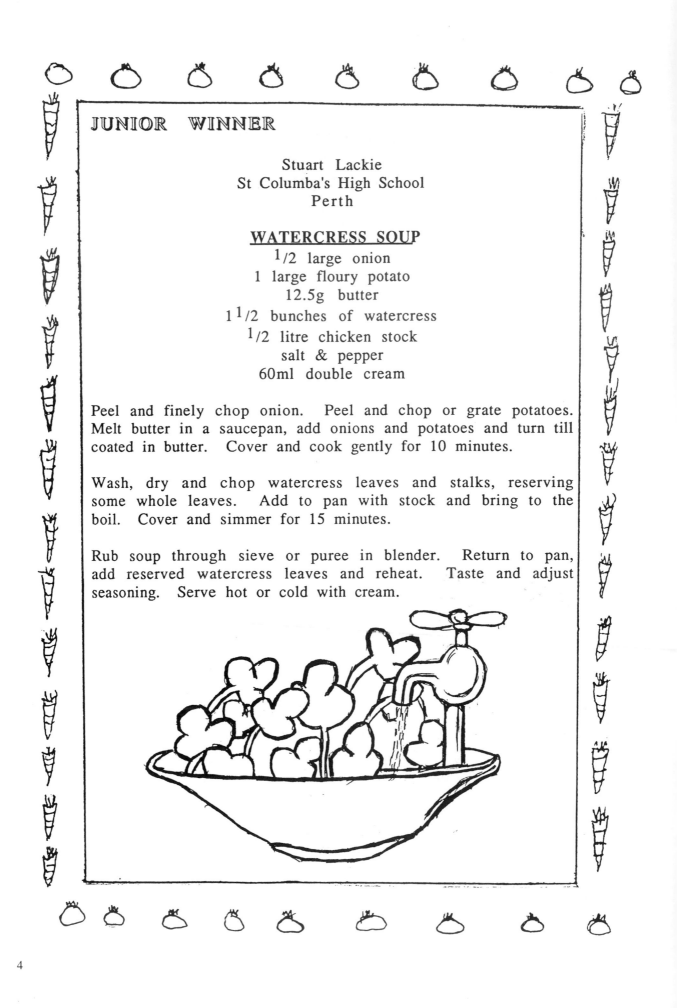

JOINT THIRD PRIZE

Bridgend of Teith
Doune

FRESH ASPARAGUS MOUSSE
Serves 8 - 10

3 bunches fresh asparagus
(or 2 tins green asparagus)
1 packet aspic jelly powder
3 egg whites
$1/2$ generous pint boiling water
seasoning
sherry or wine vinegar to taste
$1/2$ pint double cream

Cook the fresh asparagus tied together in bunches in a pan with boiling water and foil wrapped round the tops, till ready.
Cut off enough tops for your decoration and liquidise the rest.
Dissolve the aspic in just over $1/2$ pint boiling water along with sherry, wine vinegar and seasoning. Leave in a cool place till nearly set. Pour a little on to the bottom of the dish or dishes you are going to use and press in the decoration of the fresh asparagus.
Whip the cream, whip the whites. Mix asparagus with the aspic. Fold in the cream, and lastly the whipped whites. Leave to set, and turn out the next day.
You may need to pop the dish for a second into boiling water, and loosen with a knife.
Garnish with tiny bunches of asparagus, steamed & tied up with a split leek leaf and soaked in French dressing;

Caroline Stroyan

JOINT THIRD PRIZE

Ray Kuhn
19 Rowanbank
Scone

MATTJES HERRING SALAD

6 Mattjes herring fillets, cut into small pieces
1/2 - 1 onion (according to taste) chopped
400g (i.e. 3 - 4) apples, peeled and diced
125g sweet and sour gherkins, diced
parsley and 1/2 stick of celery, chopped (celery optional)
3 - 4 tablespoons mayonnaise
1 teaspoon mild French mustard
salt and pepper to taste

Ingredients to be mixed and left to stand for some hours before serving with fingers of buttered bread or toast.

~ ~ ~ ~ ~ ~ ~

JOINT THIRD PRIZE

Martha Spencer
'Master Chef of 1992'
Airlie Castle
Kirriemuir
Angus

CHICKEN LIVER PATE
Serves 12-14

1 pound chicken livers
2/3 cup thinly sliced onions
1 clove garlic, peeled and crushed (1/2 teaspoon)
2 bay leaves, crushed
1/4 teaspoon thyme leaves
8 oz water
2 teaspoons salt
3/4 pound unsalted butter, softened
freshly ground black pepper
2 teaspoons Cognac

1. Place the livers, onions, garlic, bay leaves, thyme, water and 1 teaspoon salt in a saucepan. Bring to a boil, cover, and cook at a bare simmer for 7 to 8 minutes. Remove from the heat and allow to cool.

2. Take out the solids with a slotted spoon and place them in a bowl of a food processor with metal blade. Start processing the liver, adding the butter piece by piece. Finally, add the second teaspoon salt, the pepper, and Cognac and process for 2 more minutes so that the mixture is very creamy and completely smooth.

3. Pour into a mould. Decorate with chives and tomato skin and glaze with aspic if desired. Refrigerate and serve with Melba toast.

Dollar Road
Tillicoultry

ROASTED ITALIAN PEPPERS

Allow 1 pepper per person - Red/green/yellow.
Cut in half lengthways.
Remove seeds, leaving stalk intact.
Lay in greased shallow baking tin and into each half put:
some fresh basil (1 leaf)
2 - 3 slices garlic
2 small pieces of skinned tomato
1 anchovy fillet cut into pieces
1 dessertspoon of virgin olive oil
freshly ground black pepper.
Cook in hot oven 350°F/180°C or Top Roasting over Aga for about 30-40 minutes.
Leave to cool and serve in dish with fresh basil/parsley scattered over.
Use good bread e.g. Ciabatta to mop up the juices.

Jane O'Dell

7

Lady Sarah Walter
Westwood
Balthayock
by Perth

CUCUMBER AND CHEESE MOUSSE
Serves 6

1 large cucumber

1 teaspoon onion juice

1/4 pt of boiling water or (soaked in

        chicken stock cold water)

2 tbsp white wine vinegar

Pinch of mace or coriander

Brown bread and butter

6 oz curd or cream cheese

Salt and white pepper

1/2 oz gelatine

3 tablespoons of sugar

1 tablespoon of castor

1/4 pint double cream (lightly whipped)

For garnish: One bunch of watercress
For sauce: 1/4 pint of french dressing
       1 large green pepper (to serve separately)

First oil a ring mould. Peel and dice the cucumber very finely, sprinkle with salt and leave it pressed between two plates for 30 minute. Work cheese with onion juice and seasoning. Pour boiling water (or stock) on to soaked gelatine, stir until it is dissolved, then add cheese.

Drain the diced cucumber really well, and mix with the vinegar, sugar and spice. When the cheese mixture is quite cold, fold in the cucumber, add the cream. Pour into the prepared mould and leave to set in the fridge.

Chop the green pepper, blanch into boiling water and refresh in cold water. Turn mousse out and fill the centre with watercress. Add the green pepper to the french dressing, and serve with brown bread and butter.

Silla Keyser
cake-maker 'par excellence'

Essendy House
Blairgowrie
tel. 0250 884313

TROUT MOUSSE made out of
CHOCOLATE CAKE
! ! ! ! !

1 lb fresh trout

1/2 pint milk

Bay leaf

Onion

1 oz butter

1 oz plain flour

1/4 pint mayonnaise

1/4 pint double cream

1/4 pint cold water

1/2 oz gelatine

1 tbsp lemon juice

Salt & pepper

Bake the trout in foil and butter. When cooked, allow to cool and remove all skin and bones. Infuse for 20 minutes milk, bay leaf and peeled onion. Melt the butter, mix in flour and gradually stir in infused milk, making a smooth sauce. Season with salt & pepper. Cover and leave until cold. Work trout until smooth and add to cold sauce.. Measure cold water and sprinkle over gelatine. Soak for 5 minutes and stir over low heat to dissolve. Add mayonnaise to trout and cold sauce, stir in gelatine with the lemon juice and fold in lightly whipped cream. Decorate with thinly sliced cucumber.

Silla's amazing entry to the Starter Party was actually made entirely of chocolate cake but with a recipe - exquisitely written in icing - for a trout mousse. We subsequently very successfully raffled the 'cake' (to the benefit of the Charity) which looked like this:

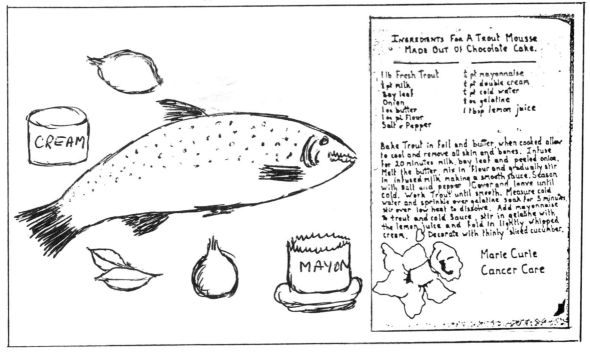

John Webber's
Filo Pastry Flan of Courgette and Tomato Seasoned with Feta Cheese and Basil
(Serves 4)

4 sheets of Filo Pastry
Olive Oil
4 Courgettes
6 Tomatoes (Plum if possible)
4 dsrt spns Pesto Sauce
6 oz Feta Cheese
Garlic
Basil
Sea Salt and Mill Pepper

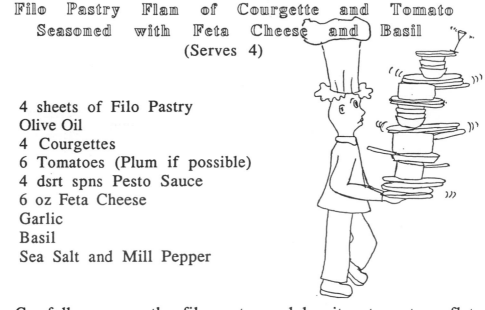

1.   Carefully unwrap the filo pastry and lay it out on to a flat surface and cover with a cloth to avoid the paste drying out. Take the first sheet off the stack, place alongside and brush lightly with the olive oil.   Cover with another sheet of pastry and repeat until you have a piece of pastry three layers thick and covered in oil.

2.   Cut out disks of pastry using a saucer or small plate the size you wish the finished flan to be, and cutting around with the point of a sharp knife.   Arrange the disks on to a baking sheet and put aside.

3.   Top, tail and wash the courgettes, then slice thinly.   Pour some of the oil into a large shallow pan and half cook the slices by tossing in the hot oil with a clove of garlic for flavour.

4.   Carefully lay the courgettes in circles on the pastry disks, slightly overlapping each other and allowing approximately a quarter inch border from the edge.

5.   Skin and deseed the tomatoes and carefully dice the flesh. Place a spoonful of the tomato flesh in the centre of each flan and season with a spoonful of the pesto sauce.

6.   Cut the feta cheese into quarter inch dice and sprinkle over the tomato mixture.

7.   Bake the flans at 375-400F for 8-10 minutes.   Garnish with freshly cut basil and serve at once.

Kinnaird House Hotel

The Post House
Lethnot
Brechin, Angus

SMOKED FISH MOUSSE
Serves 4 - 6

12 Whiting fillets - skinned
1 tblspn lemon juice,
7 fl oz double cream
1 (size 3) egg white, whisked till thick
1 tblspn chopped fresh tarragon
1 tblspn chopped fresh parsley

$^{1}/4$ oz gelatine
4 oz smoked salmon or trout
salt & pepper

1. Poach the whiting with the lemon juice in enough water to cover for approx. 10 minutes.
2. While the fish cools, measure 3 tblspn of the poaching liquid & dissolve gelatine in it.
3. Puree fish & gelatine mixture coarsely in a food processor. Stir in cream.
4. Oil 4 ramekin dishes, cut 4 circles of smoked salmon to fit bottoms & place one in each ramekin. Chop the trimmings and add to the fish mixture.
5. Fold egg white into the fish mixture with the herbs. Season to taste and spoon into the ramekins. Chill until set.
6. Arrange salad of your choice on plates.
7. Loosen mousse from sides of each dish, unmould onto salad.
8. Chill until ready to serve.

Note A fruity salad is nice with the mousse. Depending on size of ramekins you may get 6, so cut 6 rounds of smoked salmon for bottoms.

Mrs Lily Gibb

These two recipes are from the Patients at
MacMillan House
Perth

MARINATED KIPPERS
Serves 6

1 large onion - sliced + bay leaves
2 cured kippers (boneless)
Marinade:
1 gill vinegar + a few peppercorns
1 teaspoon dry mustard

Method
Skin & slice kippers (finger size)
Lay sliced onions & bayleaves on top.
Pour over marinade, leave to marinate overnight.
Strain well and serve with brown bread & butter.
* * * * * * * *

SMOKED HADDOCK PATE

1 pr smokies	Ground black pepper
2 oz butter	Cream or yogurt to mix
1 dessertspn lemon juice	

Method
Skin & bone smokies
Flake & put in large bowl
Add lemon juice, pepper, 1 oz butter and cream or yogurt
Mix well together
Spoon into ramekins
Melt remaining 1 oz butter and pour over mousse.

Serve with toast triangles

19 Rowanbank
Scone

Ray Kuhn

* * * * * * *
GARLIC MUSHROOMS
Serves 4

4 rashers streaky bacon	125g cream cheese with garlic & herbs
125g mushrooms	1 small tub (142g/5 fl oz) whipping cream

Cut the bacon into small pieces and fry till crisp.
Chop the mushrooms and add to the bacon.
When cooked, mix in the cream cheese and enough cream to make a thick sauce.
Divide the mixture between 4 ramekins and place a thin slice of mushroom on top of each one.
Before serving place under grill to heat through and brown slightly.

C. Watt
c/o Boots the Chemists
High Street
Perth.

MUSHROOM TARTS
Serves 4

8 oz mushrooms (mixed variety for preference)
1 large onion   (finely chopped)
1 oz butter
2 fl oz whisky
4 oz puff pastry (ready made is fine)

Fry onion gently in butter until soft.
Add chopped mushrooms, whisky and freshly ground pepper and salt to taste, and cook, stirring until mushrooms have reduced in bulk and are fairly dry. Allow to cool.
Roll out pastry fairly thinly and cut into 4" circles.
Put in large shallow patty tins and brush edges with egg wash.
Fill with cooked mushroom mixture.
Bake at 230°C for 20 25 minutes.
Dust with chopped parsley
    and serve hot or warm.

Ursula Mackenzie

Auchleeks House
Calvine
Pitlochry

SCALLOP & SALMON CEVICHE
with TOMATO VINAIGRETTE
(serves 4)

1 x 8 oz fillet of salmon, skinned	2 teasp white wine vinegar
4 large or 8 small scallops (shells removed)	fresh basil
Juice of 1 large lemon	Salt & pepper

Slice salmon into very thin, neat slices
Separate the scallop corals:
Slice scallop meat into 2 or 3 thin discs, depending on size
Arrange in one layer in china dish with salmon slices.
Drizzle over lemon juice and white wine vinegar
Sprinkle with a few torn basil leaves
Season with freshly ground salt & pepper
Cover dish with cling film and leave in a cool place to marinate for 20-30 minutes.
Meanwhile, heat a knob of butter in a small pan and fry off the corals for about $1/2$ minute.
Cook and cut into two, lengthwise
Drain fish from marinade and place decoratively on serving plate with cooled corals and a few salad leaves.
Coat with tomato vinaigrette made as follows:

1 small clove of garlic, crushed	Pinch of sugar
6 tablespoons good olive oil	$1/2$ shallot, very finely
$1^1/2$ tablespoons white wine vinegar	chopped
Freshly ground salt & black pepper	

Put all into screw top jar and shake to amalgamate.
Mix with 3 tomatoes, peeled, seeded and finely chopped
some fresh chopped parsley and finely torn basil leaves.

WATERCRESS ROULADE
Serves 6

6 oz watercress
4 eggs (size 3) - separated
1 tbsp plain flour
pinch of salt

Mrs Katherine Duff
11 Queens Court
Queens Avenue, Perth

Filling:
8 oz carrots (chopped)
Juice of 1 orange
8 oz cream cheese
$1/4$ teasp ground nutmeg

To garnish:
Shreds of orange rind or grated carrot
Watercress sprigs

Set oven at 200°C (400°F, Gas Mark 6) Lightly oil a 7 x 11 inch Swiss roll tin and line with non-stick baking parchment.

Place the watercress in a pan with 3 tbsp water. Cook, covered, for 5 minutes. Drain and blend with egg yolks, flour and salt until the watercress is finely chopped.

Whisk the egg whites until stiff and fold into the watercress mixture.

Spoon into tin and bake for 15 minutes until firm and springy.

Carefully turn out onto a sheet of non-stick baking parchment, peel away lining paper and roll up from one short side with the parchment inside. Allow to cool.

Filling: Place carrots in a pan with orange juice and simmer, covered, until carrots are almost tender.

Remove lid and cook carrots until tender, allowing liquid to evaporate.

Puree carrots with the cream cheese and nutmeg until smooth.

Un-roll the roulade, remove parchment and spread with the filling to within $1/4$ inch of the edge. Re-roll. Serve cut into thick slices, garnished with shreds of orange rind or grated carrot and watercress and sprigs.

FISH SAUTE WITH HAZELNUT TOPPING

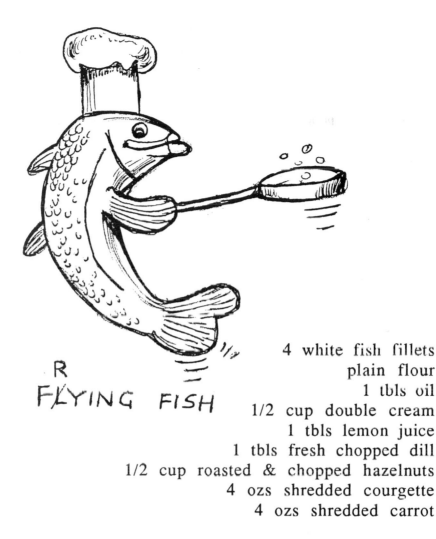

R
FLYING FISH

4 white fish fillets
plain flour
1 tbls oil
1/2 cup double cream
1 tbls lemon juice
1 tbls fresh chopped dill
1/2 cup roasted & chopped hazelnuts
4 ozs shredded courgette
4 ozs shredded carrot

Toss fish in flour, shake away the excess flour. Heat oil in pan, add the fish and cook for about three minutes on each side until golden brown. Drain on a piece of kitchen roll and keep warm. Add cream, lemon juice, dill and hazelnuts to fish juices in pan and stir over a medium heat until the sauce thickens.

Microwave the shredded courgettes and carrots. Season and place fish with sauce topping on top of courgette and carrot mixture.

Katie Targett-Adams
27 Heriot Row
Edinburgh

C R O S T I N I

Ciabatta bread
Aubergine
Red Pepper
Artichoke Hearts
Mozarella

Pesto and/or olive paste
Garlic, basil, lemon juice
Black pepper and salt
Olive oil
Parsley

Brush the sliced bread with oil and grill slightly. When cold spread a little pesto or olive paste on one side.
Roast the aubergine or char grill with oil, when cooked cover with more oil, lemon juice, parsley and black pepper. Grill and skin the red pepper and slice when cooled. Marinate the mozarella in oil and cover in basil.
Pile all the ingredients on top of the Ciabatta, decorate and plate.

Everything can be prepared well in advance.
Many alternatives can be used, i.e. Parma ham, marinated mushrooms, goat's cheese grilled on the top, sun dried tomatoes etc.

If Ciabatta is not available a french stick or tomato bread can be used.

Annie   Fraser
Rotmell
By Pitlochry

STRATHTAY SAVOURY TARTLETS
Serves 16 as a Starter or 8 as a Main Course

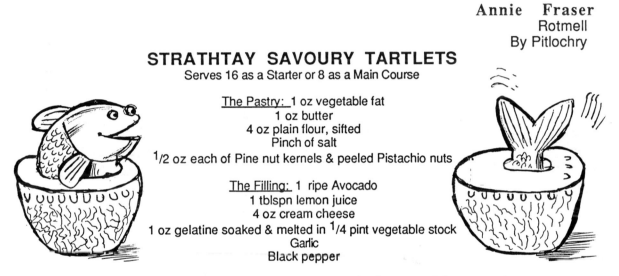

The Pastry: 1 oz vegetable fat
1 oz butter
4 oz plain flour, sifted
Pinch of salt
1/2 oz each of Pine nut kernels & peeled Pistachio nuts

The Filling: 1 ripe Avocado
1 tblspn lemon juice
4 oz cream cheese
1 oz gelatine soaked & melted in 1/4 pint vegetable stock
Garlic
Black pepper

Finishing Touch: Tombuie smoked venison (cut in slivers & artfully arranged)

First roughly grind the nuts for the pastry in the food processor. Add all the other pastry ingredients, mix well, bind with ice cold water. Chill the pastry wrapped in greaseproof paper for 1/2 hour.

Select 16 shaped pastry moulds or patty tins.
Roll out pastry 1/8" thick.
Press into tins and trim excess pastry.
Line with pieces of bakewell paper and baking beans.
Bake in hot oven for 15 mins.
Remove paper and beans, return to oven for further 15 mins.
Cool well before removing from tins.

Place all ingredients for the filling in the food processor and mix until creamy and smooth.
Place in tartlets directly and leave to set, OR allow to set then pipe filling in.
Finish with Smoked Venison.

OTHER SUGGESTIONS: half pitted black olives - smoked salmon - cherry tomatoes - anchovies
Glaze of aspic could be added to give extra special finishing touch.
Tomato passata could be used to flood plate for dinner party - good colour contrast.

SALUTATION HOTEL

34 South Street
Perth

Tel no: 0738 630066

GAME AND HERB SAUSAGE TERRINE

$1 \frac{1}{2}$ lb mixed pheasant and rabbit
$\frac{1}{2}$ lb sausage meat (PORK)
1 oz mixed herbs
3 eggs (size 3)
1 onion
$\frac{1}{2}$ oz Pistachios
$\frac{1}{4}$ lb bacon (BACK)
1 glass Brandy

COOKING UTENSIL - $\frac{1}{2}$ lb Bread Loaf Tin

Melt butter and place in mould.
Line mould dish with bacon
Mince game mix (or ask butcher to do it for you)..
Add eggs, brandy and finely chopped onion.
Mix sausage meat and herbs together.
Half fill mould with game mix.
Roll sausage meat and herbs and place in centre of mould.
Chop Pistachio nuts and sprinkle on both sides of sausage meat.
Cover sausage meat with rest of game mix
Cover with lid or tin foil.
Place in oven and cook for 40 minutes at 190°C or Gas mark 6
Chill to serve.

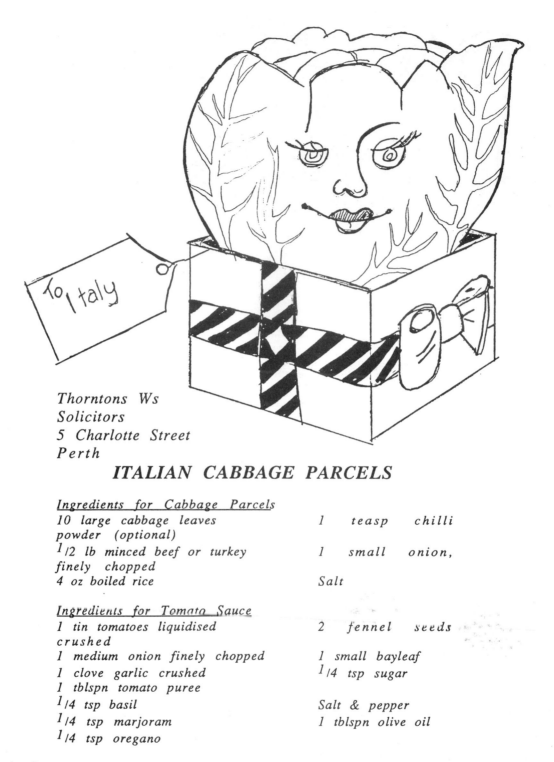

To Italy

Thorntons Ws
Solicitors
5 Charlotte Street
Perth

ITALIAN CABBAGE PARCELS

Ingredients for Cabbage Parcels

10 large cabbage leaves
powder (optional)
$1/2$ lb minced beef or turkey
finely chopped
4 oz boiled rice

1   teasp   chilli

1   small   onion,

Salt

Ingredients for Tomato Sauce

1 tin tomatoes liquidised
crushed
1 medium onion finely chopped
1 clove garlic crushed
1 tblspn tomato puree
$1/4$ tsp basil
$1/4$ tsp marjoram
$1/4$ tsp oregano

2   fennel   seeds

1 small bayleaf
$1/4$ tsp sugar

Salt & pepper
1 tblspn olive oil

To make Sauce;

Heat the oil in a medium sized saucepan, add the chopped onion and garlic. Fry the onion until soft, then add all other ingredients, stir well. Simmer for 1 hour. Remove the bayleaf.

To make the Parcels:

In a heavy based pan, fry the mince and onion together. When it is thoroughly browned, add the chilli powder and salt with just enough water to allow it to cook without sticking or burning. Simmer gently for approx. 30 mins or until the mince is cooked. Drain off any excess liquid. Once cooked, add the boiled rice and stir thoroughly. Allow to cool completely.

Remove any thick pieces of stalk from the cabbage leaves, this can be done by cutting a "V" shape out of each, then immerse them in a large pan of boiling water. Boil them only for around 5 mins as this is only to make them pliable, not to cook them completely. Drain in a colander and cool by pouring cold water over them.

You are now ready to stuff the leaves.

Place a tblspn of the stuffing in the centre of each leaf, then gently fold the edges over the mixture and roll carefully into a parcel.

Place them in a casserole dish with the flap underneath, placing them close together to stop them unrolling. Pour over the tomato sauce, cover and place in a pre-heated oven at 190C/450F/Gas mark 8 for 45 minutes.

Serve with garlic bread or buttered crusty bread.

Mrs Elizabeth Glenn
Liff
Dundee

CREAMS OF CHICKEN WITH TARRAGON & PINK GRAPEFRUIT

1 Chicken breast
1 egg yolk (size 3)
4 tblspn double cream
  segments pink grapefruit
1 clove garlic
1 1/2 teasp dried tarragon
Salt & pepper

For the Sauce
1/2 small onion, chopped
1 stick of celery, chopped
1 garlic clove, chopped
1 dessertspn butter (or marg!)
5 tblspn double cream
3 teasp grapefruit juice
Salt

Put breast, garlic, grapefruit segments, egg yolk, cream into food processor and pulverise.
Add salt & pepper to taste, and tarragon.
Grease 10 small pattie tins, or 6 medium ramekins, spoon mixture into tins, put in a Bain Marie. Place in oven for 20 mins. at 180°C

Make the sauce by softening the onion, celery and garlic in the butter. Add the cream and simmer for 3 mins. Remove from heat, add the grapefruit juice. Serve either cold as a Starter or hot with new potatoes and asparagus as a main course.

To serve as a Starter: Place on a bed of blanched sorrel leaves, pour round the sauce, add the remaining grapefruit segments and some herbs.

Healthier options: Use olive oil margarine and "Elmlea" cream.

MUSHROOM BRIOCHES

Serves 8-10

8 - 10 brioches
1 pint double cream or 2 pints single (more or less)
1 onion - chopped finely
2 double handfuls of mixed mushrooms

  e.g. oyster mushrooms
     shiitake mushrooms - tough
     field mushrooms - tough
     button mushrooms - tough

4 rashers of bacon - chopped
1 clove of garlic - minced
oil or butter
chopped parsley - 1 bunch

Softly saute garlic in oil or butter - add onion.
Saute onion in oil or butter until clear - use low heat.
Add bacon & fry until cooked.
Add sliced, tougher more robust mushrooms for flavour to impregnate cream (to be added later).
Cook through & pour in cream.
Boil until desired consistency is achieved (i.e. gets thicker - not too thin as will run out of brioche, not too thick as will clog the palate.)

NB If the sauce is reduced too much, add water to start again and boil.

Just before desired consistency is achieved, add the more delicate mushrooms that have been previously sauteed in butter.
Continue boiling until correct consistency.
Add portion of chopped parsley here for flavour.

BRIOCHES:
  Remove top & set aside for lid.
  Hollow out body using sharp small knife.
  Place in oven on low heat & warm through
   until slightly crispy.

Garnish:
Bitter lettuce e.g. lollo rosso, oak leaf, endive (well
  washed!) with French dressing of oil, vinegar
  and garlic.

To assemble:
Fill brioche with sauce & mushrooms so that it spills
  over onto plate.
Arrange garnish of lettuce in a flourish at side of
  plate & sprinkle with parsley.

Janet Scott
Oliverburn
Balthayock
by Perth

Bridgend of Teith
Doune
Perthshire

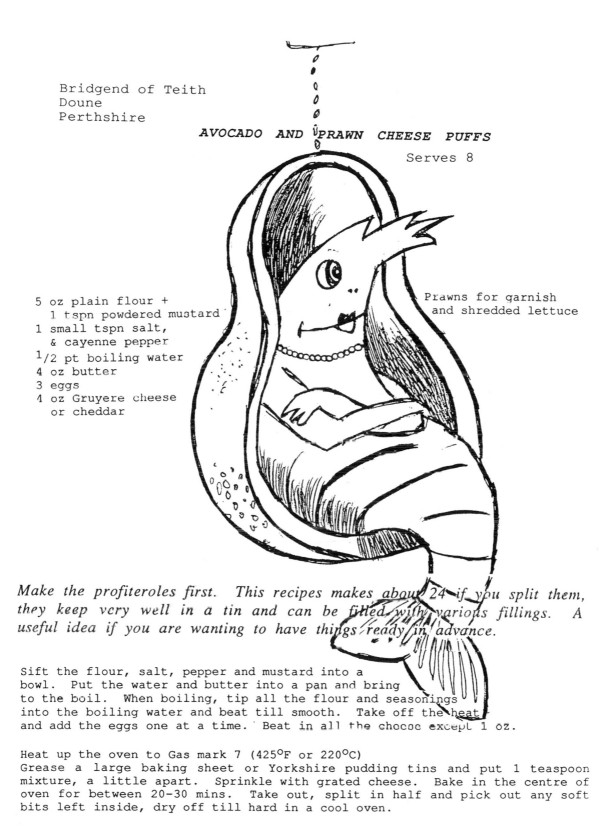

AVOCADO AND PRAWN CHEESE PUFFS

Serves 8

5 oz plain flour +
   1 tspn powdered mustard
1 small tspn salt,
   & cayenne pepper
1/2 pt boiling water
4 oz butter
3 eggs
4 oz Gruyere cheese
   or cheddar

Prawns for garnish
and shredded lettuce

Make the profiteroles first. This recipes makes about 24 if you split them, they keep very well in a tin and can be filled with various fillings. A useful idea if you are wanting to have things ready in advance.

Sift the flour, salt, pepper and mustard into a
bowl. Put the water and butter into a pan and bring
to the boil. When boiling, tip all the flour and seasonings
into the boiling water and beat till smooth. Take off the heat
and add the eggs one at a time. Beat in all the cheese except 1 oz.

Heat up the oven to Gas mark 7 (425°F or 220°C)
Grease a large baking sheet or Yorkshire pudding tins and put 1 teaspoon
mixture, a little apart. Sprinkle with grated cheese. Bake in the centre of
oven for between 20-30 mins. Take out, split in half and pick out any soft
bits left inside, dry off till hard in a cool oven.

Filling 2 Avocado pears or more if necessary.
         3 tbsp mayonnaise, garlic, lemon juice, black pepper

Mix to a smooth paste and pop into warm crispy shells, garnish with prawns and
lettuce.

Caroline Stroyan

21

Jean McIntyre
Abbey Road
Scone

PRAWN & CREAM CHEESE PATE
Serves 4 - 6

400gm cooked prawns
400gm cream cheese with herbs & garlic
1 teaspoonful lemon juice
Salt & pepper to taste
Cucumber, tomato & lemon for garnish

Place cream cheese, lemon juice, salt and pepper in a bowl and beat well. Add cooked prawns and mix through. Garnish with a twist of cucumber and wedges of lemon and tomato.

Serve with a crusty bread roll or melba toast.

Hazel   Barber

Mains of Bonskeid
Pitlochry

HAGGIS STILLAIG

Approx $1^1/2$ fresh Haggis
1 oz butter
3 tbsp chopped fresh chives (or 1 chopped clove of garlic)
Freshly ground black pepper
Pinch Salt
$1/4$ cup (at least) whisky, warmed
6 tblspn single cream

Skin haggis. Warm 6 ramekins in oven. Turn on the grill.
Very gently heat the butter and add haggis, stirring all the time. When hot, add $2/3$ chives (or all the garlic), pepper and salt to taste. Then add the whisky. This should flame mildly, (if it doesn't, light it to flambe!). When flame dies down transfer to the ramekins and pour over cream (1 tblspn per ramekin).
Brown lightly under the grill without allowing it to dry out. Remove from grill and garnish with rest of chives, if used. Serve hot.
This can be served with hot buttered toast, but I serve it on its own using a teaspoon!

Mrs. F. Hunter
38 High Street
Auchterarder

HUNTER'S   PATE
(serves 4)

1 lb chopped chicken livers
6 oz cooked ham
1 onion, chopped finely
1 clove of garlic, chopped finely
3 oz butter

2 tbsp olive oil
3 tbsp whisky or sherry
3 tbsp single cream
salt & pepper

Lightly fry the onion and garlic until soft. Add chicken livers, seasoning and fry until cooked. Put into a food processor with the cooked ham, cream and whisky. Blend for a few seconds. Refrigerate for 2 or 3 days before serving. This pate also freezes well. Serve with fingers of toast or oatcakes.

HARLEQUIN MOUSSE

2 tbsps lemon juice
1/4 pt double cream
salt
pepper

2 tbsps French dressing (approx)
1 pt mayonnaise
1/2 cucumber, diced finely with skin
4 oz smoked salmon, chopped finely
1 sachet gelatine

Lundie House
Lundie
Angus

Oil thoroughly the mould that you are going to use for this recipe. Having made my French dressing in the liquidiser, using mustard, garlic, sugar, salt, pepper, cider vinegar and sunflower oil, I make my mayonnaise, leaving some of the French dressing at the bottom of the liquidiser for added flavour. I use one egg to half a lemon, whiz it round and then add my sunflower oil until it thickens.

Dice the cucumber very finely, leaving the skin on, for colour and also cut the salmon very finely using a pair of scissors - much quicker. Cover the cucumber and the smoked salmon with French dressing as marinade.

Whip some cream lightly.

Dissolve the gelatine in the heated lemon juice. Let it cool slightly.

Mix together mayonnaise, cucumber and smoked salmon with the French dressing. Fold in the cream. Taste to see if it needs salt and pepper. Finally mix in the gelatine.

Transfer to mould. Leave to set, about 8 hours.

Turn out and serve with hot bread.

This is delicious and a great favourite - quick and simple to make - looks terrific and tastes yummy!

Roe Cassels

23

Sole Terrine with Fresh Herbs and Vegetables

The quantity will vary depending on the size and shape of the terrine. I have given quantities per lb of fish.

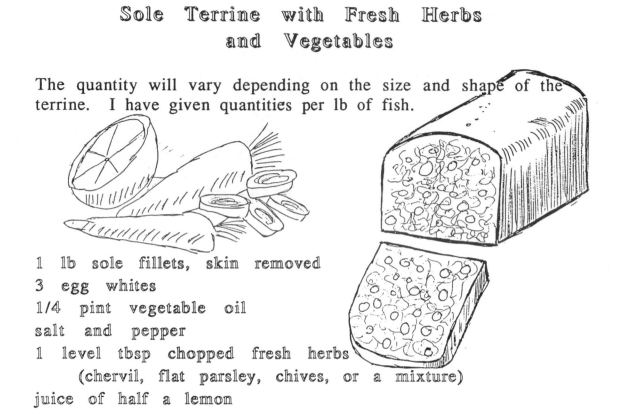

1 lb sole fillets, skin removed
3 egg whites
1/4 pint vegetable oil
salt and pepper
1 level tbsp chopped fresh herbs
    (chervil, flat parsley, chives, or a mixture)
juice of half a lemon

Method:
1. Simply chop fish into pieces & put into food processor. Work to a paste.
2. Add egg whites & mix together.
3. Add oil & process until blended together.
4. Remove from processor & pass through a sieve (by working it through with your hand or back of spoon) into a bowl. Add lemon juice.
5. Chop herbs and work through mixture. Season to taste.

To assemble:
1. Line terrine with cling film.
2. Spoon mixture into terrine until filled. Level off top with spatula.
3. Place terrine in 'bain marie' or deep tray filled with hot water. Cover with aluminium foil, put tray on heat and simmer for about 15-30 minutes until set. (Time may vary depending on size and shape of terrine, but it is not too critical providing you never let the water dry up.)

To serve:

Turn terrine out on to a board and cut into portions.   Serve with salad and some herb flavoured mayonnaise.   This dish is delicious hot or cold.

If you wish to make the terrine more interesting you can use salmon or smoked salmon using perhaps 1 lb of salmon and 2 lb of sole.   By filling the terrine in such a way you can have a pretty pattern of red and white fish.   Alternatively you can use chicken meat instead of fish, perhaps with vegetables through it.

David Wilson
The Peat Inn

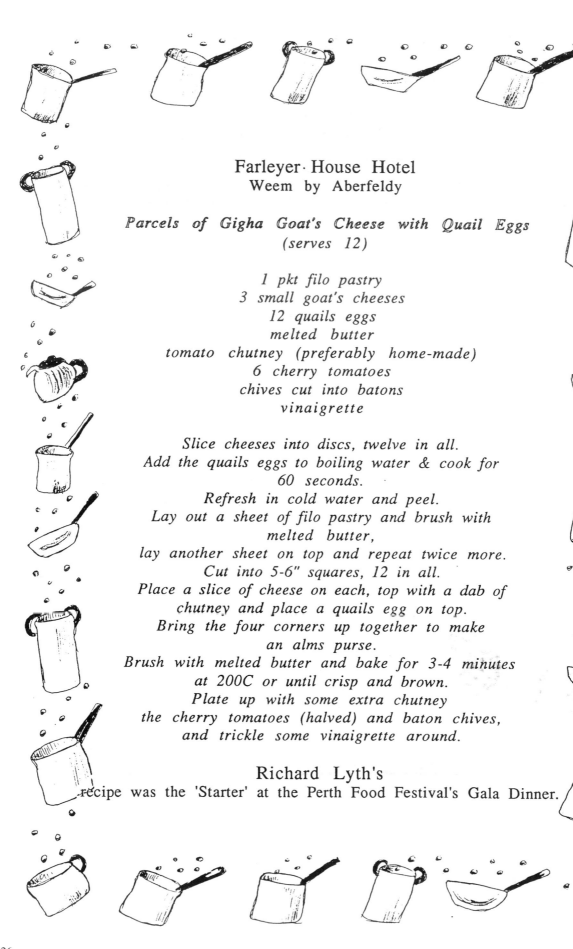

Farleyer·House Hotel
Weem by Aberfeldy

Parcels of Gigha Goat's Cheese with Quail Eggs
(serves 12)

1 pkt filo pastry
3 small goat's cheeses
12 quails eggs
melted butter
tomato chutney (preferably home-made)
6 cherry tomatoes
chives cut into batons
vinaigrette

Slice cheeses into discs, twelve in all.
Add the quails eggs to boiling water & cook for
60 seconds.
Refresh in cold water and peel.
Lay out a sheet of filo pastry and brush with
melted butter,
lay another sheet on top and repeat twice more.
Cut into 5-6" squares, 12 in all.
Place a slice of cheese on each, top with a dab of
chutney and place a quails egg on top.
Bring the four corners up together to make
an alms purse.
Brush with melted butter and bake for 3-4 minutes
at 200C or until crisp and brown.
Plate up with some extra chutney
the cherry tomatoes (halved) and baton chives,
and trickle some vinaigrette around.

Richard Lyth's
recipe was the 'Starter' at the Perth Food Festival's Gala Dinner.

Smoked cod's roe mousse

3/4 lb smoked cod's roe, skinned
1/2 pt whipping cream
2 egg whites
salt, pepper & lemon juice

Whip cream to soft peak stage. Fold in cod's roe and the beaten egg whites. Season to taste with lemon and ground black pepper and salt (only if required). Garnish (optional) with aspic and cucumber. Serve with brown bread and butter.

The Hon. Mrs. F.G. Gillies
Kilmany
Cupar

THE PROVOST'S
SALMON MOULD

8 oz boiled or tinned salmon
2 beaten eggs
3 oz margarine
3 tbsp fresh breadcrumbs
salt & pepper to taste

Melt margarine. Mix with frothy eggs. Blend in the flaked salmon, then the breadcrumbs.
Put in shaped greased mould or dish & steam for 45 minutes or bake for 30 minutes. Serve hot or cold.

Mrs Jean McCormack
Perth & Kinross District Council
2 High Street, Perth

27

Easter Dunbarnie
Bridge of Earn
Perth

The Hon. Mrs. Ranald Noel-Paton's
AVOCADO MOUSSE WITH SUN-DRIED TOMATOES
Serves 4

2 large avocados
Juice of 1 lemon
$^1/4$ pint chicken stock
$^1/2$ oz gelatine
2 cloves garlic, chopped
3 tblspn fromage frais

2 tblspn mayonnaise
Basil leaves, torn up
3 tblspn sun-dried tomatoes
  chopped into smallish pieces
Salt & pepper

Scoop out flesh of avocados and liquidise together with lemon juice. Put chicken stock in a saucepan and sprinkle on the gelatine, heat gently until gelatine has dissolved.
Add this to the avocado mixture, plus the garlic, salt and pepper and blend together, finally adding the fromage frais and mayonnaise.
Fold in the sun-dried tomatoes and basil to the whole mixture (but no more whizzing)
Pour into mould and chill.
De-mould before serving and add some fresh basil leaves for decoration.

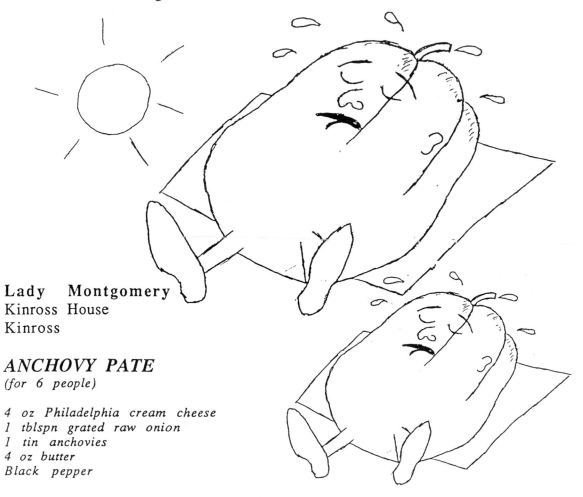

Lady Montgomery
Kinross House
Kinross

ANCHOVY PATE
(for 6 people)

4 oz Philadelphia cream cheese
1 tblspn grated raw onion
1 tin anchovies
4 oz butter
Black pepper

*Drain the oil from the anchovies & put them in the Magimix
or food processor with all the other ingredients.
Mix until smooth and serve with hot brown toast or rolls.*

Kate Leathley
From a recipe suggested by
MISS BOYNE
Sandra Court, Perth

SOLE & SALMON ROLLS WITH HOLLANDAISE SAUCE

Lay a piece of smoked salmon on top of a piece of lemon sole and roll firmly.

Wrap in greased foil and bake in oven for approx. 20 mins at 180°C, 350°F, Gas Mark 4.

Serve with hollandaise sauce and garnish with lemon wedge and parsley.

Finlarig
Luncarty

HOT & SOUR PICKLED PRAWNS
Serves 4

Ingredients
16 large prawns (peeled)
2 fl oz cider vinegar
1/2 yellow pepper, thinly sliced
Juice of 2 lemons
1/2 red pepper, thinly sliced
1 dessertspn Tabasco sauce
1 red onion
1 dessertspn Worcestershire sauce
1 tblspn drained capers
1/2 level teasp salt
1 lemon thinly sliced
Freshly ground black pepper
5 oz olive oil
1 level teasp sugar
1 level teasp dry mustard

Method
Mix all ingredients in a 1 3/4 pint polythene box. Leave for at least 48 hours in the refrigerator. Give contents a shake from time to time - remove from refrigerator half an hour before serving. Serve the prawns with plenty of the marinade poured over and lots of your favourite bread to mop up the juices.

Kathleen Blyth

MOUSSELINE OF SOLE WITH PRAWNS
(for 8)

450g (1 lb) Fillets of Sole - skinned and chopped
 50g (2 oz) Shelled prawns
1 egg white, beaten
1/2 teasp salt
1/4 teasp ground white pepper
15 oz double cream

3 egg yolks
3 oz unsalted butter
 (softened)
2 teasp lemon juice
1 teasp tomato puree

Peggy Thomson

To garnish: whole prawns

1. Combine the chopped fish with the prawns, egg white and seasoning. Puree the mixture in a blender or food processor with 10 fluid ozs of cream.

2. Oil six ovenproof ramekins and press the mixture well down into the dishes. Cover each dish with a round of foil pleated in the centre. Chill for 3 hrs.

3. Place the ramekins in a large roasting tin, and half fill with boiling water. Bake in the oven at 150°C (300°F) Mark 2 for 30-40 minutes. Stand on a wire rack to drain. Keep warm.

4. Over a pan of hot water combine yolks, a knob of butter and lemon juice. Whisk until thick. Remove from heat, add remaining cream whipped, return to heat, without boiling. Turn out, add sauce and garnish.

**Durley Dene Crescent
Bridge of Earn**

Fiona Goldthorpe

CAULIFLOWER, SMOKED CHEESE & MUSTARD SOUP
Serves 4

12 oz cauliflower
2 pts chicken stock
1/4 pt single cream
4 oz smoked cheddar
1 tbsp wholegrain mustard
salt, pepper, nutmeg
1 oz plain flour
1 oz margarine
1 onion
1/2 leek

Sweat onions and leek in margarine for 2 - 3 minutes.
Fold in flour and mix before adding hot stock - bring to boil.
Add cauliflower and simmer until tender. Liquidise.
Grate cheese into soup and add cream.
Add mustard. Season and finish with cream swirl.
Serve hot.

POTAGE SOLFERINO

Battle of Solferino - 24th June 1859

White part of large leek (roughly chopped)
2 oz onion (roughly chopped)
1/2 lb potatoes (roughly chopped)
3/4lb tomatoes (peeled & cored)

Cook in vegetable stock for 3/4 hour

Add: 1 clove of garlic (finely chopped) and 2 oz butter.

Liquidise - pass through fine sieve.
Season including a little sugar and a dash of cayenne.
Re-heat gently.

Mrs. Barbara Mackenzie
President 1984 - 1994

Mrs. Andrea Targett-Adams
27 Heriot Row
Edinburgh

Spicy Vegetables in Crispy Baskets
(making 2 ramekins)

2 sheets filo pastry
Oil

Spicy vegetables:

1 tbsp oil	2 oz mangetout
1 small onion	2 tsp soy sauce
1 med pepper	1/2 cup water +
	1 tbsp extra water
1 med carrot	2 tsp cornflour
4 oz broccoli	

Method:
Oil the outside of 2 small ramekins.
Place the dishes upside down onto a greased tray.
Cut filo pastry in half and take 2 sheets, separate them, oil both sheets and place them over dish.
Bake in moderate oven for about 5 minutes.

Spicy vegetables:
Heat oil in frying pan, add onion, fry until soft. Add all the other vegetables and stir fry for a couple of minutes. Add soy sauce and water and cook for a further 2 minutes. Blend cornflour with extra water and add to mixture. When mixture has thickened, place in baskets.

NEOPOLITAN SAVOURY MOUSSE
serves 4 - 6

4 fillets smoked haddock, cooked, & 4 hard boilded eggs
Mash well & mix with 1pt white sauce

8 oz spinach & 8 oz carrots, cooked & pureed
$1/2$ tin chopped tomatoes, pureed, and 3 sachets gelatine

Dissolve $1/2$ sachet gelatine with carrot puree. Spread on bottom of dish or tin. Set.
Dissolve 1 sachet gelatine with fish mixture & spread on top of carrot mixture. Set.
Dissolve $1/2$ sachet gelatine with tomato puree & spread on top of fish mixture. Set.
Dissolve $1/2$ sachet gelatine with spinach mixture & spread on top of tomato mix. Set.

When mousse is fully set,
turn out carefully on to a plate
and surround with garnish of your choice,
or slice & lay out on a flat dish,
showing off different colours.

Burnbank
Saline
Dunfermline, Fife

Lorna   Barr

PEARS AND STILTON

Use one ripe pear per head
(halved, peeled and cored)

Fill the cavity with softened Stilton cheese.

Put on plates, cavity down,
and
cover liberally with mayonnaise.

Decorate with a
pinch of paprika and a few bits
of chopped chives

Mrs Bruce Hamilton
Glencarse House
by Perth

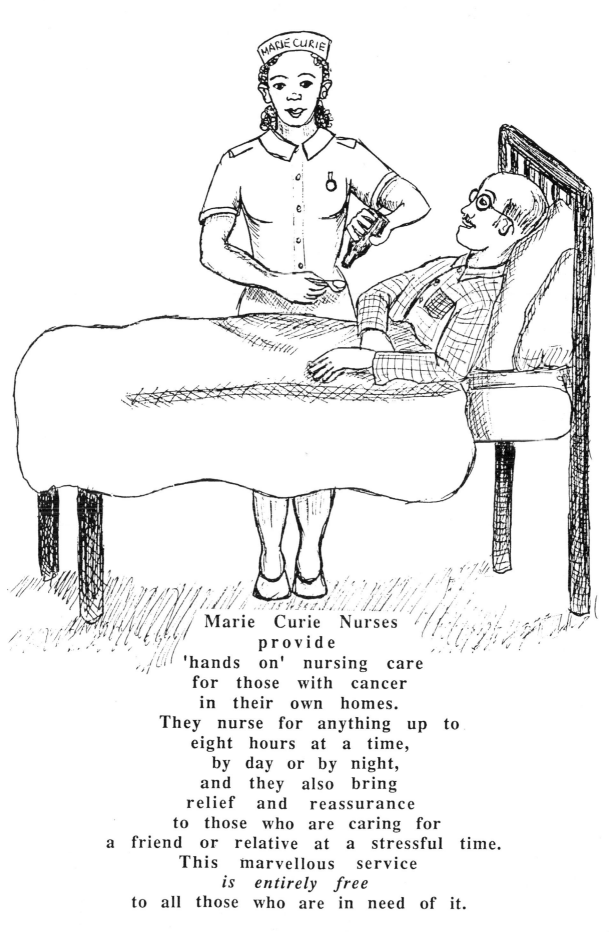

Marie Curie Nurses
provide
'hands on' nursing care
for those with cancer
in their own homes.
They nurse for anything up to
eight hours at a time,
by day or by night,
and they also bring
relief and reassurance
to those who are caring for
a friend or relative at a stressful time.
This marvellous service
is entirely free
to all those who are in need of it.

Steamed asparagus rolled in salmon and served with a shallot butter sauce
(Serves 4)

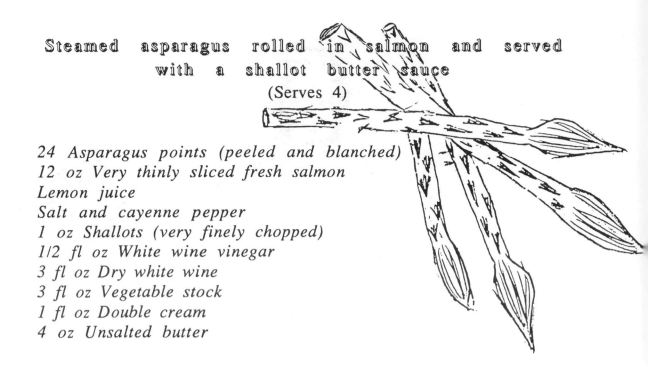

24 Asparagus points (peeled and blanched)
12 oz Very thinly sliced fresh salmon
Lemon juice
Salt and cayenne pepper
1 oz Shallots (very finely chopped)
1/2 fl oz White wine vinegar
3 fl oz Dry white wine
3 fl oz Vegetable stock
1 fl oz Double cream
4 oz Unsalted butter

Salmon skin (free of scales cut into small strips and deep fried)
Chopped chives.

Method:
Take the cooked asparagus and cut into suitable lengths for the size of plate used (I would recommend a 10" diameter plate) allowing six sticks per portion.

Carefully wrap each stick with a slice of salmon leaving about 2" of green tip showing. Set them in a steamer tray leaving a gap between each piece then set aside ready for cooking.

To make the sauce put the white wine, shallots and vegetable stock into a stainless steel pan and boil on a medium heat until the liquid has reduced by 4/5ths.

Reduce the heat and add the double cream. Return to the simmer, then move the pan to a very low heat and slowly work the firm butter into the liquid in small pieces. Season with salt, cayenne pepper and lemon juice and keep warm.

To serve, lightly season the salmon with salt, mill pepper and lemon juice, then steam for 5-8 minutes depending upon your steamer.

Arrange the cooked asparagus onto hot plates and sauce over the salmon leaving the green points showing through. Sprinkle with the deep fried salmon skin and chopped chives.

John Webber
Kinnaird House Hotel

Hot mushroom and caramalised onion and cheese sandwich

(Serve mini portions on a bed of lettuce leaves as a starter or have a larger portion for a light lunch.)

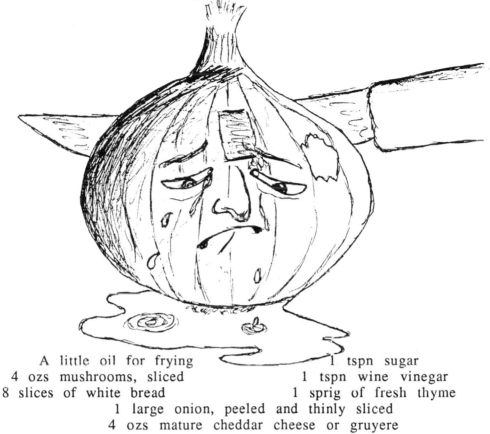

A little oil for frying
4 ozs mushrooms, sliced
8 slices of white bread
1 large onion, peeled and thinly sliced
4 ozs mature cheddar cheese or gruyere
1 tspn sugar
1 tspn wine vinegar
1 sprig of fresh thyme

Fry the onion in a little oil. When the onion starts to cook losing volume and gaining colour, add the sugar. Stir well and cook for 2 minutes. Add the vinegar, stir and cook again for a further 2 minutes. Add mushrooms and fry gently until cooked. Drain off any liquid and add a few leaves of thyme.

Grill the bread on one side, turn over the bread and sprinkle the cheese on the untoasted side. Return the bread to the grill until the cheese melts.

Fill the sandwiches with caramelised onion and mushroom mixture and serve straight away.

Katie Targett-Adams
27 Heriot Row
Edinburgh

Lawton
Burrelton

FISH, SPINACH & WATERCRESS TERRINE WITH CURRIED MAYONNAISE AND GRAPES
Serves 4

1 lb sole, skinned & filleted
2 egg whites
7 fl oz double cream
Salt & green peppercorns
4 tblspn cooked & drained Spinach,
   (fresh or frozen)

$1/4$ pint mayonnaise
1 tblspn creme fraiche
1 teaspn curry powder
Handful of seedless, peeled grapes
Fresh Dill for garnish
4 tblspn chopped watercress

Pound sole in food processor with small amount of lightly beaten egg white. Turn into bowl and fold in the rest of the egg white and the double cream. Season with salt and milled green peppercorns.

Butter a terrine or loaf dish and line with greaseproof paper. Fill with one-third of fish mixture, then a layer of chopped watercress. Follow with another layer of fish, then spinach, and finish with final layer of fish. Smooth with a spatula, and place dish in roasting tin half filled with not quite boiling water. Put in oven pre-heated to 350°F (180°C, gas mark 4), and bake for about 40 minutes. Take from oven and allow to cool before turning out on to plate.

Make quarter-pint good HOME MADE mayonnaise and beat in tablespoon of creme fraiche and one teaspoon medium curry powder (the curry taste should not be too strong),

Put two tablespoons of mayonnaise on each serving plate and slice of terrine on top. Garnish with dill on sauce and scatter grapes over all.

Morag Henderson
On behalf of SAVE THE CHILDREN

Meriel Hoare
Blue Cottage
Lower Froyle
Alton, Hants

TRICOLOR d'ECOSSE
(Vegetarian)

2 crushed oatcakes
2 crushed sesame seed Ryvita
$1 1/2$ oz melted butter

ADD TOGETHER AND PRESS INTO SHAPE - PUT IN FRIDGE

2 carrots (steamed) - mixed with curry paste
4 mangetout/sugar snap peas - mayonnaise to bind.
Large cupful of steamed cabbage and carroway seeds - onion & garlic pulp

Steam and mash 3 vegetables. Add seasoning and a little binder of your choice (i.e. as suggested above). Heap onto base individually, thereby making three layers, and decorate.

Mary Rose Reville
17 Greenside Court
St Andrews

BLUE CHEESE AND PEAR TARTLETS
Serves 6

<u>Pastry</u>

4 oz plain flour
4 oz wholemeal flour
2 oz butter
3 tbsp water

<u>Filling</u>

$3^1/2$-4 oz blue cheese (Lanark, Beenleigh,
    Cashel, Roquefort, whichever you prefer)
1 oz walnut pieces
2 oz diced pear
$^1/4$ pint single cream
2 tbsp milk
2 eggs
sprigs of thyme

To prepare the pastry sift flour into a bowl and rub in chopped butter until a breadcrumb consistency is achieved. Mix in just enough water to make a fairly stiff dough. Roll out and line 6 fluted flan tins (4 - $4^1/2$ inches across) Blind bake at 400°F (200°C) gas mark 6, for 20-25 minutes. Toast the walnut pieces during the last 8-10 minutes on a lower shelf.

Divide the toasted walnuts among the tartlet cases. Break the cheese into chunks and add to the tartlets together with the diced pear and sprinkle with thyme leaves.

Season the eggs and mix in the milk and cream. Pour a little into each tartlet and bake at 375°F (190°C), gas mark 5, for 20 minutes until the egg mixture is just set. Allow to cool for about 5 minutes before serving. Garnish with watercress leaves.

Kenneth Nicol
"Muircroft"
Western Road
Auchterarder

SUMMER SEAS ROULADE

3 eggs
1 oz tinned leaf spinach (drained) or
a few leaves of fresh spinach, in season
salt and pepper
1 oz finely chopped onion
1 oz butter (for frying)
1 oz smoked salmon
1 oz prawns
very small piece of green chilli, finely chopped (optional)

Melt butter and fry onion and chilli until soft. If using tinned spinach, drain, heat in pan or microwave and place in warmed oven to remove some of the moisture.

Meanwhile, make up omelette mix - whip together 3 eggs and seasoning.

When onion mixture is soft, add prawns and omelette mix. Cook omelette until ready to fold and remove from heat.

Place a fine layer of spinach up the middle of the omelette. On top of this layer of spinach, place slices of smoked salmon and a further layer of spinach. Fold omelette over spinach, like a roll. Turn onto plate and leave to cool and refrigerate for 3-4 hours. When cool, use a very sharp knife and slice thinly (approx. 1cm thick) Place on a starter plate.

Garnish with assorted leaves and serve with mild curried chutney and walnut bread.

Sward Cottage
Moredun Terrace
Perth

Mrs Alison McLeod

CHILLED MELON SOUP
(serves 4)

1 melon over 2 lb
5 oz granulated sugar
8 fl oz dry white wine
5-10 fl oz soured cream or creme fresh
lemon juice

Strip melon to $1^1/2$ lbs of melon flesh.
Dissolve 1 pt water & sugar over a low heat, simmer for 4 - 5 mins. Cool.
Liquidise melon & wine.
Gradually add syrup.
Stop adding when it suits taste.
Add lemon juice if required.
Add cream.
Chill and serve.

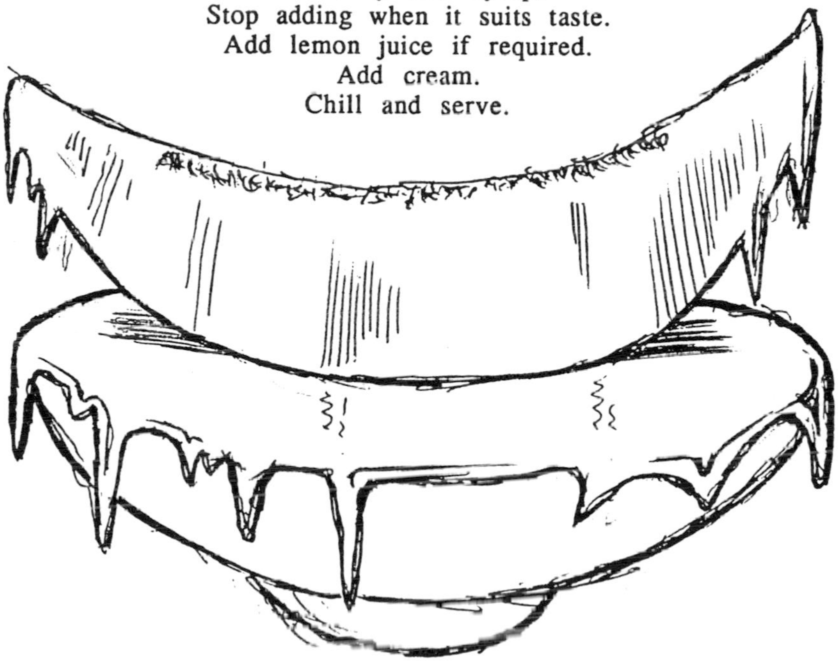

Gail Barclay
1 Rocheid Park
Edinburgh

CREAM CHEESE STUFFED AVOCADOS

Firm avocados
Cream cheese
Black olives

Chives
Juice of 1 lemon

Method
Cut pears lengthways - remove stones and peel.
Soften cream cheese with a little cream.
Season with chives (chopped) and chopped pitted black olives.
Fill cavity of each pear.
Press 2 halves together. Brush each with lemon juice & wrap in waxed paper & chill.
Serve cut in slices across the pears on shredded lettuce with a good French dressing.

*   **Keep avocado green by placing whole pear into boiling water for 5 seconds, then peel.**

43

Mrs. M.H. Gow
Drummonie
Bridge of Earn
Perth

STUFFED TOMATOES or AVOCADOS
Easy - Prepare ahead - Serves 6

2 cups tinned artichoke hearts, chopped
$1/2$ cup celery, chopped
$1/2$ cup spring onion, chopped
$3/4$ cup mayonnaise
Bacon - cooked and crumbled
Salt - pepper - squeeze of lemon.

Combine first 4 ingredients
Stuff tomatoes with mixture
Crumble bacon on top
Chill and serve

Glenbeich
Lochearnhead
Perthshire

Charmian Holcroft

VEGETABLE STARTER
Serves 8-ish

3 medium-sized aubergines, cut into chunky slices
6 large courgettes, cut in long thick slices
Extra virgin olive oil, allow $1/4$ - $1/2$ pint
2 red peppers, halved and cored
2 yellow peppers, halved and cored
2 green peppers, halved and cored
1 teaspoon dried mint
1 teaspoon dried dill
2 teaspoons dried oregano
1 clove garlic, crushed - optional: (add to oil if used)
Fresh salad leaves
Lightly-toasted pine kernels
Salt and pepper.

Lay the aubergines in a colander and salt lightly, then leave to drain for half an hour. Rinse well and pat dry with kitchen towel. Brush the aubergines and courgettes well with olive oil.

Heat the grill and cook the aubergines and courgettes until lightly charred, turning once or twice. Do this in relays and lay vegetables in a large shallow dish. Grill the peppers skin-side up until blackened. Leave them to cool, covered with a clean tea towel for 10 minutes, then skin and cut each piece in half again. Arrange the peppers in the dish. Trickle more olive oil over, season and sprinkle with the herbs, stirring to coat and cover. Leave for 4-6 hours to marinate. Arrange some salad leaves on an ashet, top with the vegetables and serve at room temperature. Toss the pine kernels over the salad at the last minute.

Leek, haddock and herb mousses
makes 8-10

3 leeks, trimmed
8 oz/225g smoked haddock
4 fl oz/100ml milk
1 tblspn/15ml butter
black pepper and salt
1 teaspn/5ml lemon juice
1 tblspn/15ml fresh parsley, chopped

1 tblspn/15ml fresh chives, chopped
8 oz/225g ricotta cheese
1 tblspn/15ml creamed horseradish
1 egg
10 ramekins
tomato slices, to garnish

Preheat oven to Mark 3 (325ºF, 160ºC) Chop one leek finely and place in a large frying pan with haddock. Pour over milk and dot fish with butter. Season, sprinkle over lemon juice. Place lid over pan, poach fish on top of hob over a gentle heat for 10 minutes until fish flakes easily.

Flake fish into small pieces, place in bowl with cooking liquid. Add herbs to bowl, mix well. Mix ricotta cheese until smooth, fold into bowl with creamed horseradish and egg.

Take remaining leeks and peel away strips lengthways. Bring a small pan of water to the boil and blanch the strips for a few minutes. Drain and use to line the bottom of the ramekins.

Spoon some fish mixture into bottom of each, place in a baking tray with 1in/2.5cm of water up side of dishes. Bake for 20-30 minutes until set. Cool then turn out. Garnish with tomato slices. Serve with melba toast.

DANSCOT
8 Kinnoull Street
Perth

John   Webber
Kinnaird

COD AND CRAB CAKES
WITH AN AVOCADO AND CORIANDER SALSA

The cod cakes take their origin from a both traditional British fish cake and Maryland crab cakes, combined to form a lighter, more flavourful dish.   The garlic, potato and cod also combine to produce a flavour akin to a brandade.

The Crab Cakes

6 oz Picked white crab meat

3 oz cooked cod fillet

3 oz Mashed, steamed, potato

Paprika

Zest of 1 lemon

Sea salt

2 oz shredded spring onion

1/4 oz root ginger, cut into very fine strips

1 small clove of garlic, crushed in salt

2 tblspn mayonnaise (made with olive oil)

Flour, beaten egg & sieved, dried breadcrumb
          to coat.

The Salsa

1 ripe Hass avocado

Juice of 1 lemon

Juice of 1 lime

3 med. plum tomatoes, blanched and peeled

1 shallot, peeled and cut into fine rings

1 teaspn chopped leaf coriander

1/2 oz toasted pine kernels

1 oz cucumber (cut into small balls with a solferino spoon)

1/2 teaspn yellow mustard seed (soaked overnight in white wine)

5 fl oz Virgin olive oil (use a medium range fruity oil with not too harsh a bite)

Sea salt and milled pepper

To garnish: Fish crisps and fresh dill

METHOD

1,   Carefully fold together the crab meat and potato adding the mayonnaise little by little.

2.   Add the spring onion, ginger and crushed garlic. Flake the cod fillet and add to the mix, stirring as little as possible to obtain a bound mixture.

3.   Season with sea salt and paprika as required, and add more garlic if needed.

4.   Using a dessert spoon and pallet knife portion and form the mix into eight cakes using a little flour to prevent sticking.   Pass through the egg and bread crumb and refrigerate on a tray lined with cling film.

5.   To make the salsa, quarter the peeled tomatoes and remove the pips.   Cut off any spare flesh on the inside of the tomato and cut the remainder into 1/4" dice or diamonds.   Retain the pips and flesh trimmings for use in sauces.

6.   Halve, peel and remove the stone from the avocado.   Cut the fruit into dice or diamonds the same size as the tomato.   Place into a stainless steel or glass bowl together with the tomatoes and add the lemon and lime juices.   Pour in the olive oil, and add the mustard seeds, chopped coriander, shallots, cucumber and pine kernels.

7.   Season with sea salt and mill pepper turning the mixture over very carefully to avoid mashing the avocado.   Let the mixture stand for at least 30 minutes before use but do not make more than can be used in one service.

8.   To serve cook the cakes in clarified butter until hot through and a light golden brown.   Drain on kitchen paper and serve on a bed of the salsa served in a large deep plate.   Garnish with fish crisps and leaf dill.

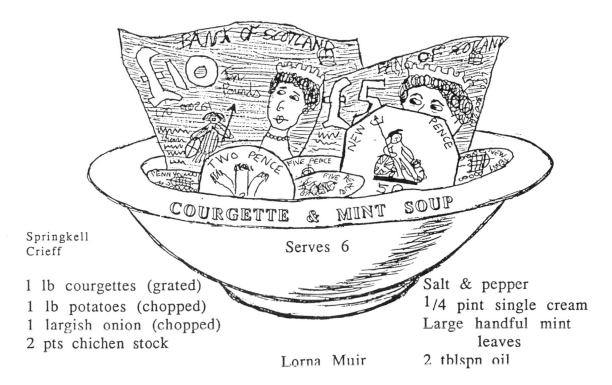

COURGETTE & MINT SOUP

Springkell
Crieff

Serves 6

1 lb courgettes (grated)
1 lb potatoes (chopped)
1 largish onion (chopped)
2 pts chichen stock

Salt & pepper
1/4 pint single cream
Large handful mint
leaves
2 tblspn oil

Lorna Muir

"Sweat" the potatoes and onion in the oil until onion transparent - then add hot chicken stock. Cook until potatoes are soft. Add the courgettes. Cook for a further 10 minutes. Add salt & pepper, cream and then mint leaves and put in food processor.   Can be served hot or cold.

Brian J Mackie
KINROSS HIGH SCHOOL

CARROT AND ORANGE SOUP (Serves 4)

Can be served HOT or COLD

1 medium onion - chopped
50g (2oz) butter
450g (1 lb) carrots, diced
1 litre (1 3/4 pints) chicken stock

Juice of 1 1/2 oranges
100ml (4fl oz) single cream
Grated rind of 1 orange
Salt & pepper

Melt butter in a large pan and gently fry the onions until soft.
Add the diced carrots and chicken stock.
Bring to the boil.
Simmer for 20 minutes until the vegetables are tender.
Remove from heat and puree in a blender or food processor.
Return to the pan and add the orange juice, rind and single cream.
Season to taste.
Reheat without boiling.

47

SMOKED SALMON STAR
with a Dill and Sour Cream Sauce
for 2 people

7 oz smoked salmon
1$\frac{1}{2}$ oz unsalted butter
2 teaspn lemon juice
2 tblspn single cream
pepper

Sauce ingredients:
$\frac{1}{4}$ pt sour cream
pinch celery seed
pinch garlic powder
2 tblspn fresh dill, chopped

Mixed leaves to garnish
Caviar to garnish (optional)

Using 3 oz of smoked salmon -
Cut up the smoked salmon pieces, reserving wide, flat pieces out of remaining 4 oz salmon for the star, and place in food processor.
Melt the butter and mix with lemon juice and cream. Add this to the salmon in processor.
Blend the mixture and season with pepper. Spoon into a small round mould and refrigerate until set.

FOR THE STAR
Draw a star about 6" wide (15cm) on greaseproof paper. Cut out one of the legs of the star as a template and use it to cut out 5 equal legs for the star shape out of 4 oz salmon. Lay the flat salmon pieces on a plate in a star shape leaving a space in the middle for the mousse. Place mousse in middle of star and garnish top with a small amount of caviar or lumpfish roe. Arrange mixed leaves around mousse and serve with dill and sour cream sauce.

FOR THE SAUCE
Mix all the sauce ingredients together and chill.
Let stand no longer than 2 hours.

Katie   Targett-Adams
27 Heriot Row
Edinburgh

26 Albany Terrace
Perth

POTAGE DE POISSON FUME
Best served hot
Serves 4 - 6

This is not a critical recipe. Its common name i.e. "fish soup" is offputting
to most people but, without exception, everyone who has tried it has come back
for more. Here then is my suggestion for an extremely tasty starter. We have
had this hot and cold (with various accompaniments) but I would suggest this
be taken as a hot soup.

8 oz smoked haddock fillets   *Paprika*
4 oz haddock fillets   *1 - 2 cloves garlic (optional)*
1 onion (medium size)   *Any other seafood available*
Some button mushrooms   *(e.g. prawns, scallops, clams)*
Some butter   *Also peas, sweetcorn etc.*
Some milk   *A suitable stock can be made from cubes*
                                         (fish or chicken)

Place fish in a steamer or between two plates on a pan of boiling water.
Add a few knobs of butter, a little milk, and sprinkle with paprika. Steam
for around 15 minutes, save liquid and flake fish (not too small pieces).
Chop vegetables fairly finely and lightly fry (a wok is ideal).
Put the whole lot into a suitable pot, with water as necessary, add any other
seafoods and simmer gently for a few minutes.
If you decide to add vegetables such as carrots, peppers and the like, it will
require longer cooking or, alternatively, they would be better cooked
separately.

As I said at the start this is an extremely tasty starter and has been enjoyed
by many guests over the years.

Bon appetit!   Mr. T.J.W. Ross

Ann I McIntyre
Luachmhor
Kinfauns
Perth

ROOTI TUTTI SOUP

Serves 4 - 6

1 tbsp grapeseed oil
2 onions
1 clove of garlic
2 leeks
1 sweet potato
6 Jerusalem artichokes
1/4 celeriac

2 stalks celery
1 kohl rabi
1 courgette
1/2 tsp ground cumin
1/2 tsp ground coriander
1 litre chicken (or light vegetable) stock
Salt & freshly ground pepper

Gently fry the chopped onion in the oil in a large saucepan for a few minutes. Then add the other chopped vegetables and the herbs. Cover the pan and sweat the vegetables for 10 minutes. Next add the stock. Bring to the boil and simmer for 40 minutes or until the vegetables are soft.

Let the soup cool, then liquidise it thoroughly, making sure it is completely smooth. Season well with salt and pepper and reheat the soup gently.

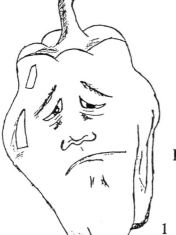

Mrs. Ian Petrie
RUTHVEN MILL
By Meigle

R E D   P E P P E R   S O U P
6 servings

2 oz unsalted butter
1 lb onions, peeled and finely sliced
1 1/4 lb red peppers, cored and seeded

3 fl oz dry sherry
grated rind of one orange
1 tablespoon caster sugar

1 level teaspoon ground coriander
1 pint orange juice (freshly squeezed)
Seasoning

Garnish
Teaspoon fromage frais or yoghurt

Melt butter in thick pan, add onions and cook until softened.
Remove stalks and seeds from peppers. Slice finely or use food processor.
Add peppers and remaining ingredients to onions, cover and simmer gently for 45-60 mins. Liquidise and then sieve into rinsed out pan. Reheat and correct consistency. Season to taste.

Serve hot in warm bowls. Garnish.

Claire Macdonald's
Tomato & Horseradish Creamy Jelly with Crab & Rice Salad
(serves 6)

8 tomatoes, skinned, halved & de-seeded
2 cloves of garlic, poached for 1 minute then skinned
1/2 pt stock - chicken or vegetable
3 tspns horseradish
salt & freshly ground black pepper
2 tspns Worcester sauce
1 sachet gelatine (1/2 oz)
8 oz Philadelphia cheese

Warm the stock and dissolve the gelatine granules
in it - take care not to let it boil. Cool.
Rinse out a small ring mould with cold water.
Put the skinned and de-seeded tomato halves into a
food processor and whizz to a puree. Still whizzing,
add the skinned poached garlic cloves, the cooled
gelatine and stock, the horseradish, worcester sauce
& philadelphia, salt and pepper. Pour this into the
ring mould and leave to set. To turn out dip briefly
in warm water to loosen the jelly, and turn onto a
serving plate.

Fill with the crab and rice mixture:

1 lb crab - white and brown meat mixed
4 oz cooked basmati rice (I cook it in
chicken stock for a bit more flavour)
3 tbls good mayonnaise
2 tbls mixed chopped parsley and snipped chives.

Barbara Mackenzie's
WALNUT & SPRING ONION TARTS

Filling:
3 oz Philadelphia cream cheese
3 fl oz double cream
1 teasp sugar
3 pinches cayenne
3 egg yolks
1 bunch spring onions
   (chopped, using as much green as possible)
2 oz chopped walnuts & a pinch of salt

Pastry:
6 oz plain flour
1/2 teasp salt
4 oz butter
1 egg white

Pastry
Sift flour & salt into bowl. Add melted butter - mix well.
Add egg white - stir until smooth.
Stand aside to cool for 5 mins.
Divide warm dough into 16 balls.
Press them into patty tins to line them,
bring edges up a little higher than the rim.
Refrigerate for half an hour at least.
Set oven at Gas mark 5 (375°F).

Filling
Whisk cream & cheese together,
then whisk in egg yolks thoroughly.
Season with sugar, cayenne and salt.
Stir in chopped spring onions and walnuts.
Spoon into lined patty tins.
Cook in centre of oven until rich brown.
Leave to cool in tins for a few minutes.
Serve warm on bed of lettuce leaves.
Re-heat if made in advance.

Mayfield
Forgandenny

52

Julian Perera
St Columba's High School
Perth

MUSHROOMS IN PORT

Double Cream (2 x 15ml spoon)
Onion ($1/2$)
Tiny Button Mushrooms (175g)
Butter (65g)
Port (2 x 30ml spoon)
Bread (2 slices)
Salt & freshly ground pepper

Melt 25g of the butter in a frying pan. Add the onions and fry
gently until soft.
Add the mushrooms and continue cooking for 2 to 3 minutes.
Stir in the port and salt and pepper to taste and simmer for 3 minutes.
Add the cream, reheat gently and adjust the seasoning.
Serve hot on pieces of bread fried in the remaining butter.
Garnish with parsley.

Lady Montgomery
Kinross House
Kinross

LAYERED FISH MOUSSE
For 8 people

8 oz or 4 pieces of Haddock or Whiting	$1/2$ pint Milk
4 oz of Salmon or Sea Trout	Lemon juice
5 oz Butter	Watercress or Parsley
2 oz Plain flour	Black pepper
8 ox carton Double Cream	1 Sachet of Powdered Gelatine

Separate the haddock fillets removing the backbone and any other bones you can feel, put these bits in a saucepan with a little of the milk and simmer. Put the haddock in an ovenproof dish with an ounce of butter and the remains of the milk and cook in a medium oven for about 15 minutes. Remove and cool.

Meantime put the salmon or trout in another dish with 2 oz of butter and quite a lot of lemon juice and again cook slowly until just cooked - about 10-15 minutes.

Melt the remaining butter in a pan, add the flour and then slowly stir in the milk from the fish. Strain the milk from the bones and add the juice from the salmon. Divide the sauce into three bowls.

Put the haddock in a Magimix and process until smooth and put an equal amount into two of the bowls.
Dissolve the gelatine in a little water - cool and then whip the cream.
Mix the salmon in the same way and add to the third bowl, seasoning well with salt, black pepper and lemon juice.

Lastly, Magimix or chop finely quite a lot of parsley or watercress and mix into the next bowl of fish. Divide the gelatine between the three bowls and mix well, then do the same with the whipped cream and make sure that each bowl is properly seasoned.

You can either divide the mixtures into a ring mould starting with the salmon, then the watercress and lastly the plain - turn it out when set and fill with prawns or salad or alternatively do the same in a loaf tin - turn it out and serve with a lemon hollandaise sauce

KATE LEATHLEY
Glenfield Cottage
Harrietfield

MELON WITH ELDERBERRY

frozen filo pastry	melon balls
5 fl oz elderberry cordial	1 rounded tsp ground arrowroot

Use filo pastry as per instructions on packet. Line patty or similar tins to create desired shape. Bake blind.
Heat elderberry cordial, mix arrowroot with a little cold water, add cordial, return to pan, bring to boil and remove from heat. Can be used hot or cold.
Place melon balls in pastry cases and spoon sauce onto plate.

QUAIL'S EGG & WALNUT SALAD
Serves 6

Rossie
Forgandenny

12 Quails eggs - boiled for 3 mins, peeled
1 inch of ginger, finely chopped
50gms of walnuts, finely chopped
3 cloves garlic, crushed
Juice of $^{1}/2$ lemon
Salt & Pepper
Olive oil
6 oven baked squares of bread
   brushed with olive oil
Lemon flavoured home-made mayonnaise

Mix the ginger, walnuts, garlic, lemon juice and oil together to a paste.
Spread on fried bread and place 2 eggs halved on top.
Finish with a coat of mayonnaise.
Garnish with any salad. I use coriander leaves, French beans and baby corn.

Judy Nichol

Mrs. C. Dunbar
"Balloburn"
Abernethy

SMOKED SALMON TARTLETS
ROASTED RED PEPPER SAUCE
Makes approximately 1 dozen

Pastry

4 oz plain flour	1 dessertspn lemon juice
2 oz hard margarine	$1/2$ dessertspn cold water
or butter	salt & pepper

Method

Sift flour into food processor with seasonings.   Rub in margarine until texture of fine breadcrumbs.   Pour in liquid.   Mix to stiff dough.   Roll out very thinly.   Cut into rounds and line patty tins.   Chill $1/2$ hr.

Filling

1/4 pint double cream	6 oz smoked salmon trimmings
1 egg + 1 yolk	little pepper & sprigs of dill

Method

Shred salmon.   Place in tartlets.

Whisk cream & eggs and season.   Bake moderate hot oven (180°C) until just firm to the touch.

N.B.   A better result is achieved if the patty tins are placed on already hot baking sheets.

ROASTED RED PEPPER SAUCE

2 red peppers
1 shallot - peeled & chopped finely
4 ripe tomatoes, skinned, seeded
   and chopped
1 garlic clove, peeled & crushed
1 tbls olive oil
4 fl oz vegetable stock
salt & pepper
1 oz unsalted butter

Method

Bake peppers in oven (200°C) until dark spots appear
   on skins - about 8 mins.   Cover for 3-4 mins. then skin,
   core & chop.
Sweat shallots & garlic in olive oil until softened.
Add chopped tomatoes and cook for approx. 5 minutes.
Transfer to blender & puree.   Return to pan.   Correct seasoning & consistency.
Whisk in butter and serve or leave to cool.

N.B.   It is preferable to serve tartlets warm on cool sauce.

The Garden House
Balthayock
Perth

HOT SMOKED TROUT

1 smoked trout per person
Lettuce - Lemon - Butter

Skin trout, leaving head and tail on.

Wrap in 2 or 3 lettuce leaves & bake in silver foil in
pre-heated oven (180°C) for 12 minutes.

Serve immediately and cover with a hot lemon and butter sauce.

DELICIOUS!   Belinda Pinckney

CREAMY CHICKEN MOUSSE
Serves 8

1 lb cooked minced chicken
15 fl oz thick Bechamel sauce
3 large eggs, separated
3 tblspn fresh dill (finely chopped)
1 teasp grated nutmeg
2 dashes Tabasco sauce
Salt & ground black pepper
1$\frac{1}{2}$ oz gelatine

Bechamel sauce (to make 15 fl oz)
2$\frac{1}{2}$ oz butter
3 tblspn chopped onion
3 tblspn chopped ham
3 tblspn flour
22$\frac{1}{2}$ fl oz milk (I use Jersey milk)
1 bay leaf
6 peppercorns
$\frac{1}{2}$ chicken stock cube
Salt & pepper

Melt butter in pan and saute onion till soft.
Stir in finely chopped ham and flour. Cook for 2 - 3 mins, stirring constantly.
Add stock cube, bay leaf, peppercorns to milk. Bring to boiling point and allow to infuse for 10 minutes. Strain. Add hot milk to flour roux, gradually until sauce thickens. Season. The Bechamel sauce is now ready for use in the recipe.

Mousse - Mix minced chicken with Bechamel sauce. Beat in egg yolks, dill and nutmeg, tabasco and seasoning.
Sprinkle gelatine over 4 tablespoons cold water in a bowl. Set bowl in pot of simmering water until gelatine is dissolved. Add gelatine to chicken mixture, beating well. Whisk egg whites until stiff. Fold into chicken mixture. Pour into oiled 2 pint ring mould.
Leave to set 4 - 5 hours. Turn out and decorate as wished.

Mrs Janice Shepherd
82 Perth Street
Blairgowrie

Mrs Ann Wimberley
Foxhall
Coupar Angus
Perthshire

MELON BALLS, SHRIMPS
AND
CUCUMBER IN MILD CURRY SAUCE

Take a small quantity (about $1/4$pt) of a good
curry sauce, and when cool add to it about $1/2$pt of
good quality mayonnaise (ie, Hellmans), together with
2-3 tablespoons of whipped cream.

Cut out "ball" shapes from a **ripe** melon,
peel the half cucumber and cut it into fairly small dice.
Gently fold into the curry mixture,
together with about 3 oz shrimps.
Refrigerate until required
(best not to do this dish too far in advance).
Serve with puff pastry cut into rounds or fingers.

A delicious first course for a summer dinner party.

Norma Butcher
"Holmlea"
St Madoes

PASTA PRAWN COCKTAIL
Serves 2

2 oz cooked pasta shells
1 oz prawns
1/2 eating apple (unpeeled, chopped)
1/2 stick of celery (sliced)
1 dessertspoon "Waistline" Salad Dressing
1 dessertspoon   Tartare Sauce
1 dessertspoon Tomato Ketchup
Lettuce Leaves
Paprika Pepper
Parsley Garnish

Cook the pasta shells in boiling salted water, to which a little sunflower oil has been added (prevents the pasta sticking) for 10-12 minutes.   Drain pasta shells well & rinse in cold water.
Mix the salad dressing, tartare sauce & tomato ketchup together.
Add the cold pasta shells, prawns, chopped apple and sliced celery to the dressing and mix well together.
Line a large wine glass or similar container with shredded lettuce, pile the pasta mixture into the glass, sprinkle with paprika and add a parsley garnish.
Serve with fingers of buttered brown bread.

Leonie Nichol
BUTTERSTONE SCHOOL
Arthurstone
Meigle

KHURA   CREAM
Serves4

75g (3oz) Long grain rice
25g (1oz) Sultanas
50ml (2fl oz) Single Cream
1 teasp Curry Powder
25g (1oz) Prawns
50ml (2fl oz) Double Cream
1 tablespoon Mayonnaise
1 tablespoon Tomato Ketchup

METHOD
1.   *Boil and drain rice.*
2.   *Mix together rice, single cream, sultanas, curry powder & seasoning.*
3.   *Divide into four individual serving dishes.*
4.   *Place a few prawns on top.*
5.   *Whip cream, add mayonnaise and tomato ketchup.*
6.   *Pour this sauce over prawns.*
     Serve garnished with a prawn and a slice of lemon.

Mrs. Robin Stormonth-Darling
Balvarran
Enochdhu
Blairgowrie

SHRIMP & SOUR CREAM SOUP
(serves 6-8)

1lb peeled shrimps
6 cartons sour cream
1 tbsp mint sauce
1 tin vichysoisse
1 small onion, finely chopped
Tabasco, salt & pepper

Blend sour cream,
mint sauce & vichysoisse.
Add tabasco, salt & pepper to taste.
Add onion & shrimps. Chill for 2 hours.

MANNA HOUSE
240 HIGH STREET
PERTH
Tel: 0738 638142

ITALIAN TOMATO SOUP
(Serves 4)

1 tbls olive oil
1/2 lb onions
tsp garlic
1 oz plain or wholemeal flour
1 1/2 pints vegetable stock
chopped parsley to garnish

1 lb tomatoes (peeled, & chopped) or tinned
2 bay leaves
pinch basil
1/4 pint double cream
salt & pepper

1. Heat oil in large pan, add onion and garlic and saute gently for 5 mins. Stir in flour.
2. Remove from heat and gradually stir in stock.
3. Return to heat. Bring to boil stirring continuously until thickened.
4. Add tomatoes with puree, bay leaves and seasoning to taste. Cover and simmer 30 mins.
5. Stir in cream and basil. Return to boiling point.
   Serve at once, garnished with parsley.

Mary Rose Reville
17 Greenside Court
St Andrews

BAKED CAMEMBERT WITH GOOSEBERRY SAUCE
Serves 4 persons

140g (5oz) frozen, canned or bottled gooseberries
1 - 2 teaspoons granulated sugar, or to taste
340g (12oz) Camembert cheese
Lamb's lettuce to garnish

Set the oven to Gas Mark 4, 350ºF or 180ºC

Place the gooseberries in a pan and cook over a gentle heat until softened and a light syrup has formed - about 3-5 minutes (take care not to overcook). Add sugar to taste and stir the gooseberries frequently. Pour the gooseberry mixture into a bowl and allow to cool.

Divide the Camembert into 4. Place on a baking tray and cook for 3-5 minutes or until just soft to touch and beginning to run. Quickly place the cheese onto individual serving plates with a spoonful of gooseberry sauce. Garnish with a little Lamb's lettuce.

Delicious served with warmed Italian focaccia bread.

HUMMUS

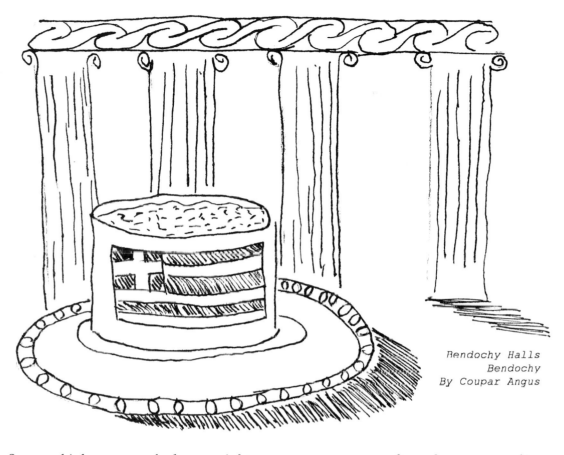

Bendochy Halls
Bendochy
By Coupar Angus

8 oz chickpeas, soaked overnight
crushed
4 tblspn tahini
3 tblspn lemon juice
2 tblspn olive oil
black pepper

3 cloves garlic,

1/4 teasp paprika
1/2 teasp salt
Freshly ground

Drain and rinse chickpeas. Place in a pan with plenty of fresh water, bring to the boil and boil for about 10 minutes. Remove to a more gentle heat and simmer for approximately 1 hour until cooked.

Drain reserving the liquid and place in a food processor. Blend until crumb-like.

Add 1/4 pint of the reserved liquid and all of the other ingredients, blend thoroughly. Leave to rest for a few hours, taste. Add more lemon juice or seasoning if required.

Dee Cameron

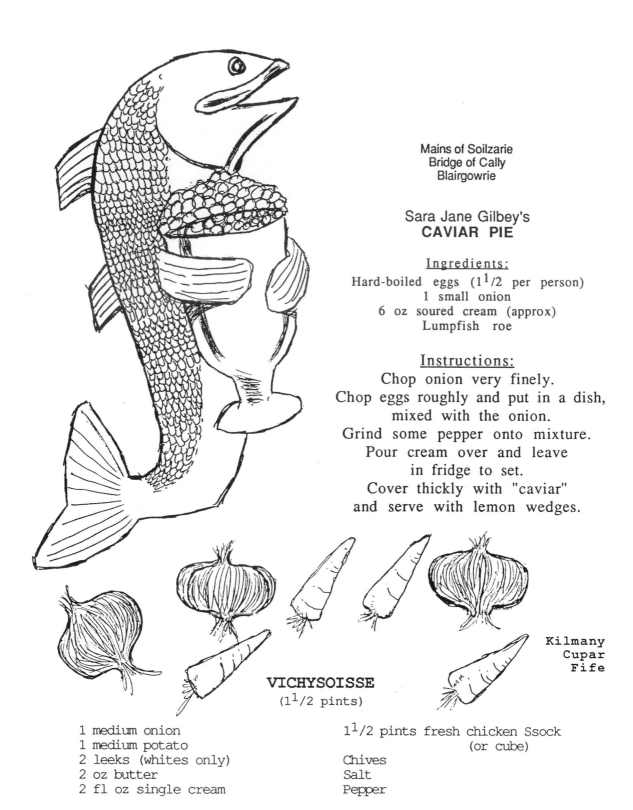

Mains of Soilzarie
Bridge of Cally
Blairgowrie

Sara Jane Gilbey's
CAVIAR PIE

<u>Ingredients:</u>
Hard-boiled eggs ($1^1/2$ per person)
1 small onion
6 oz soured cream (approx)
Lumpfish roe

<u>Instructions:</u>
Chop onion very finely.
Chop eggs roughly and put in a dish,
mixed with the onion.
Grind some pepper onto mixture.
Pour cream over and leave
in fridge to set.
Cover thickly with "caviar"
and serve with lemon wedges.

Kilmany
Cupar
Fife

VICHYSOISSE
($1^1/2$ pints)

1 medium onion
1 medium potato
2 leeks (whites only)
2 oz butter
2 fl oz single cream

$1^1/2$ pints fresh chicken Ssock
(or cube)
Chives
Salt
Pepper

Melt butter in large saucepan and saute potato and onion for 5 mins. Add the
chicken stock; bring to boil, add chopped leeks. Simmer for 40 mins and then
liquidise. Sieve, season to taste. Add cream and chives before serving (hot
or cold).

FREEZES (ungarnished)

The Hon. Mrs. F.G. Gillies

Mrs R Caffrey
13 Broom Park Crescent
Murthly

A Gateau of Smoked Trout, Tomato and Avocado
(individual portion)

Trout	skin, flake & season
Avocado	1 slice & season with lemon juice
	1 puree with mayonnaise, season
Tomatoes	concasse
	season half with basil
	other half combine with vinaigrette & place in a pot. Warm through and liquidise.
Decorate	lollo rosso, cucumber and toasted sesame seeds.

Place a cutter in the centre of plate.
Layer of flaked trout.
Layer of sliced avocado.
Layer of tomato concasse with basil.
Top with avocado mousse. Smooth off.
Remove cutter.
Sprinkle with toasted sesame seeds. Decorate,

The Garden House
Balthayock
SALLY's EGG MOUSSE
for 6

6 hard boiled eggs
1 tin Crosse & Blackwell's consomme
1/2 pt whipping (or double) cream
Worcester sauce to taste
Salt and pepper

Mix the eggs and consomme in blender reserving a little consomme for the top. Add Worcester sauce, salt and pepper. Fold in lightly whipped cream. Place in fridge for a couple of hours. Pour remaining consomme over mousse and replace in fridge until set. Decorate!

Belinda Pinckney
(This recipe has been a faithful friend to Sally Weatherall and me for a good many years, and it's still a favourite!)

65

Tim Holcroft
Glenbeich
Lochearnhead

COLD TOMATO SOUP

2 lbs tomatoes (allow about 5 tomatoes per person)
2 oz sugar
1 teaspoon salt

8 tablespoons double cream
Juice of $^1/2$ a lemon
Parsley & cucumber

Cut the tomatoes into quarters. Whiz them completely in some machine. Sieve them.
Add the cream, sugar, salt, lemon and pepper. Chill.
Salt the cucumber and dice it (having rinsed the salt off and squeezed it dry in a cloth),
and garnish the soup with the diced cucumber and chopped parsley.

Con Brid
16 Armadale Crescent
Balbeggie

Mrs. D. Radin

APPLE AND CASHEW NUT SOUP
Serves 4

1 lb carrots
1 large onion
1 small potato
1 cooking apple

2 oz butter
2 oz broken cashew nuts
2 pints vegetable stock
   (use stock cubes for speed!)

Chop the vegetables roughly and saute in the melted butter for 5 minutes.
Add the stock and nuts.Bring to the boil and simmer for 30 minutes.
Cool, blend and check seasoning. Reheat gently before serving.

Mrs Marion B Hazel
"Ellangowan"
Moigle

TUNA MOULD(s)

2 tins tuna (7oz size) - pour off liquid
2 hard boiled eggs, chopped
2 tblspn capers
1 cup mayonnaise

$1/2$ cup chives - chopped
$1/2$ - 1 cup onion - chopped
1 pkt gelatine - dissolved in
$1/2$ cup boiling water

Combine all the ingredients & press into dish (or individual dishes)
Leave to set.

Egg cup size they make ideal starters, served on salad.

Mrs Gray
23 Middlemuir Road
Stirling

CHEESE & CELERY HOT POTS
Serves 4

6 tblspn double cream
1 tblspn seeded mustard
Worcester sauce to taste

Beaten egg to mix
4 sticks of celery
4 oz mature Cheddar cheese

Cube cheese and celery finely. Mix fresh cream, seeded mustard, Worcester sauce and beaten egg together. Add seasoning and put into individual ramekin pots. Cover with tinfoil.

Cook slowly in oven in waterbath for about 20 minutes.

Mr Charles Watt
17 Mavisbank Gardens
Perth

CAULIFLOWER & STILTON SOUP
Serves 4 people

1 medium size cauliflower
1 large onion (chopped small)
$1^1/2$ oz butter
1 oz plain flour

$1^1/2$ pints chicken stock
$1/2$ pint milk
Salt & freshly milled black pepper
5 oz Stilton

Prepare cauliflower and cook for approximately 30 minutes in chicken stock.
While cauliflower is simmering, melt the butter in a saucepan, add the onion, then, keeping the heat low, allow the onion to cook for 10 minutes without colouring. Add the flour and stir to a smooth paste. Now gradually mix the milk, stirring vigorously until you have a smooth sauce. Add Stilton, turn down heat and cook for approximately 5 minutes. Add cooked cauliflower and stock to Stilton sauce and blend thoroughly (liquidise). Season with salt & pepper to taste.

Reheat and serve in warm bowls.

SENGELESE SOUP
Serves 6 - 8

1 cooking apple (chopped & peeled)
1 dessert apple   (chopped & peeled)
1 cup diced cooked chicken
3 pt chicken stock
1 bay leaf
1 cup single cream
2 oz butter
2 med. chopped onions
3 stalks celery, chopped
2 tblspn flour
1 tblspn curry powder

Lyndhurst
105 Glasgow Road
Perth

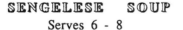

Melt butter, add onions and celery and cook till limp.
Add flour & curry and cook 2 mins. Put in liquidiser with apple, chicken and one cup stock. Blend till smooth. Put in pan with bay leaf and remaining stock, bring to boil and simmer for a few minutes. Remove bay leaf and leave to cool. Chill and add cream before serving.

This soup is also delicious hot. (If freezing, do not add cream.)

Margaret Mills

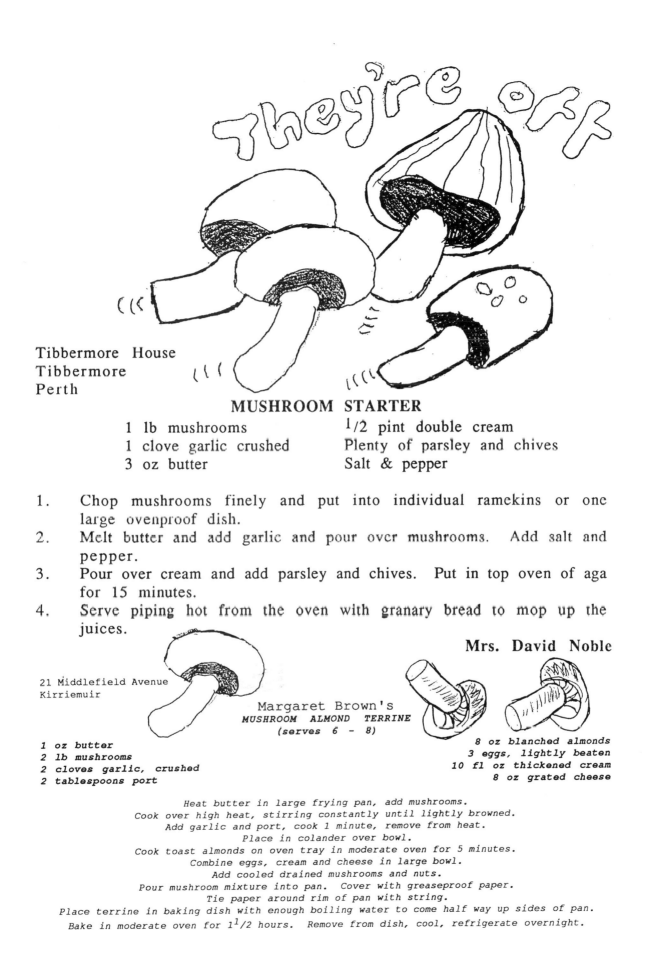

They're off

Tibbermore House
Tibbermore
Perth

MUSHROOM STARTER

1 lb mushrooms   1/2 pint double cream
1 clove garlic crushed   Plenty of parsley and chives
3 oz butter   Salt & pepper

1. Chop mushrooms finely and put into individual ramekins or one large ovenproof dish.
2. Melt butter and add garlic and pour over mushrooms. Add salt and pepper.
3. Pour over cream and add parsley and chives. Put in top oven of aga for 15 minutes.
4. Serve piping hot from the oven with granary bread to mop up the juices.

Mrs. David Noble

21 Middlefield Avenue
Kirriemuir

Margaret Brown's
MUSHROOM ALMOND TERRINE
(serves 6 - 8)

1 oz butter
2 lb mushrooms
2 cloves garlic, crushed
2 tablespoons port

8 oz blanched almonds
3 eggs, lightly beaten
10 fl oz thickened cream
8 oz grated cheese

Heat butter in large frying pan, add mushrooms.
Cook over high heat, stirring constantly until lightly browned.
Add garlic and port, cook 1 minute, remove from heat.
Place in colander over bowl.
Cook toast almonds on oven tray in moderate oven for 5 minutes.
Combine eggs, cream and cheese in large bowl.
Add cooled drained mushrooms and nuts.
Pour mushroom mixture into pan. Cover with greaseproof paper.
Tie paper around rim of pan with string.
Place terrine in baking dish with enough boiling water to come half way up sides of pan.
Bake in moderate oven for 1 1/2 hours. Remove from dish, cool, refrigerate overnight.

69

1 Packet (200g) frozen puff pastry
   (defrosted)

Gordon Sangster
Kinross High School
                Kinross

Filling
50g mushrooms, washed but
   not peeled
50g long grain rice
2 eggs
salt & pepper
beaten egg for
   glaze (optional)

PIROSHKI

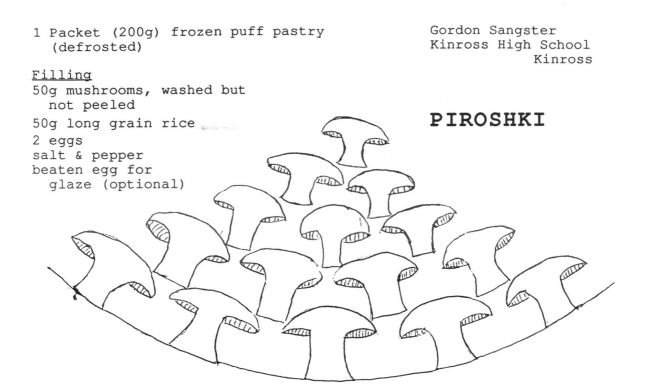

1,   Boil rice and eggs together in a pan for 10 minutes. Strain
      then cool.
2.   Finely chop the mushrooms. Peel and chop the eggs. Mix all
      the filling ingredients together.
3.   Set the oven at 220ºC / 425ºF / Gas 7.
4.   Roll out the pastry thinly on a floured surface. Using an
      8cm cutter or a glass, cut out circles of pastry. Re-roll to
      use up scraps.
5.   Put teaspoons of filling in the centre of each circle. Wet
      round the edges to seal. Brush with beaten egg if you wish.
6.   Place the crescents on a baking tray and cook for 15-20
      minutes. Serve hot or cold.

                                          Kinross High School
Gordon Sangster   Kinross

Kirkton of Liff
Liff
By Dundee

SMOKED TROUT PATE

2 FILLETS SMOKED RAINBOW TROUT   *1^1/2 TEASPN HORSERRADISH SAUCE*
2 DESSERTSPOONS CREME FRAICHE   *^{1}/4 TEASPN DIJON MUSTARD*
JUICE OF ^{1}/2 LEMON   *PEPPER*

Blend   all   ingredients   together.
Chill for 1 hour.

June   Lawson

Mrs. C. Moncrieff
Rhynd
Perth

CHEESE CREAMS

1¹/2 oz finely grated Cheddar cheese   Pinch of cayenne
1/4 pt double cream   Pinch of salt
1/4 pt double strength consomme or aspic jelly   Dash of sherry

Whip cream until stiff. Whisk consomme until frothy. Fold into cream with cheese.
Add seasoning, put into ramekins and chill.

This starter serves 4 and takes five minutes to make. It can be garnished with prawns or chives, with a little extra aspic run over the top.

'Rigifa'
College Road
Methven

A. Hart

CHICKEN LIVER & PEANUT PATE

100g/4oz butter
225g/half lb Chicken livers
1 medium onion (chopped)
1 garlic clove (peeled & crushed)
1 x 15ml spoon/1 tblspn chopped fresh mixed herbs

50g/2oz peanuts (ground)
Salt
Freshly ground black pepper
1 x 15ml spoon/1 tblsp Sherry

Melt half the butter in a pan, add the chicken livers and fry for 4 minutes, turning frequently. Remove from the pan. Add the onion and garlic to the pan and fry gently until soft. Add the remaining butter, the herbs and salt and pepper to taste, and cook for a further 1 minute. Put the chicken livers, the contents of the pan, the Sherry and the ground peanuts into an electric blender and work to a smooth puree. Smooth the mixture into six individual ramekins.

Patsy Walker
Frozen Assets
Chapelton of Balmadies
Forfar
tel: 0307 818334

Chicken Liver Parfait with Elderberry Sauce
(serves 6)

Half a small apple, peeled & cored   A clove of garlic
Half a small onion, peeled   100gr butter
200gr chicken livers   A few sprigs of rosemary
2 tbsp Calvados or brandy   Zest of a quarter orange
Salt & pepper

Melt half the butter in a large frying-pan and add chopped onion, apple and garlic. Cook gently until soft but not brown. Remove any tough sinews from the livers, cut them up roughly and add to the pan along with rosemary and orange zest. Continue to cook until the liver is done but still pink inside. Do not overcook or your end result will be rather grey and crumbly.
Liquidise until smooth, gradually adding the rest of the butter and the Calvados. Season. Pour into a mould and leave to cool. Serve with elderberry sauce, made by simmering half a pint of elderberry juice with sugar to taste. Thicken the sauce by adding a tablespoon of cornflour in a little cold water to the boiling juice, stirring the while. When the right consistency, cover tightly with cling film and leave to cool.

To serve, place a portion of parfait on each plate, spoon some sauce around it and decorate with a few seedless grapes.

These two pates have different ingredients but are processed in the same way:

Mrs David Anstice
Broomhill, Abernethy

1. PRAWN PATE

1 lb prawns, cooked, peeled & deveined
6 oz olive oil   Juice of 1 lemon
Dash of salt, pepper & paprika   chives to decorate

Mrs. Thom
20, Cluny Terrace, Perth

2. TUNA AND ORANGE PATE

1 small can tuna, drained   1 tbls double cream
Juice & rind of 1 orange

Place all ingredients in processor & puree.
Place pate in bowl & chill for 3-4 hours.

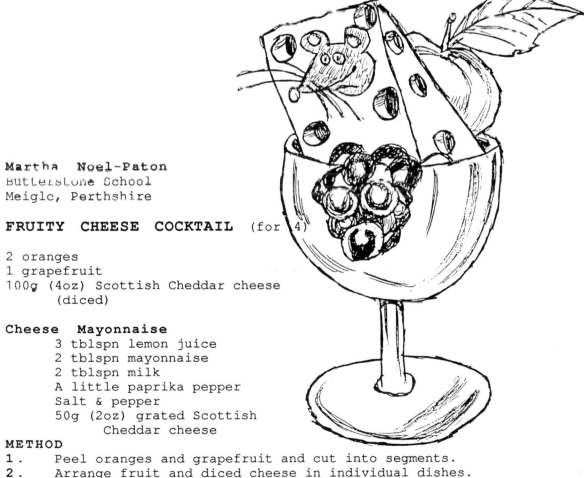

Martha Noel-Paton
Butterstone School
Meigle, Perthshire

FRUITY CHEESE COCKTAIL (for 4)

2 oranges
1 grapefruit
100g (4oz) Scottish Cheddar cheese
        (diced)

Cheese Mayonnaise
        3 tblspn lemon juice
        2 tblspn mayonnaise
        2 tblspn milk
        A little paprika pepper
        Salt & pepper
        50g (2oz) grated Scottish
            Cheddar cheese

METHOD
1.   Peel oranges and grapefruit and cut into segments.
2.   Arrange fruit and diced cheese in individual dishes.
3.   To make cheese mayonnaise, combine the lemon juice, mayonnaise, grated cheese, seasonings and milk together. Mix well.
4.   Spoon mayonnaise over fruit and cheese and sprinkle with a little paprika pepper. Garnish with a slice of orange. Serve chilled.

The Balloch
Glenisla
by Blairgowrie

CARROT MOUSSE with a prawn sauce

1 lb carrots, sliced
Pared zest and juice of $1/2$ orange
8 fl oz double cream
2 large eggs beaten
salt & pepper to taste
5 oz peeled prawns
2 tablespoons medium sherry
1 oz butter
1 extra carrot cut into julienne strips for garnish
parsley sprigs

Cook carrots in the orange juice and zest in just enough water to cover.

Liquidise to a fine puree. If too wet, reduce in a heavy-bottomed saucepan. Cool.

Pre-heat oven to 200°C/400°F, gas mark 6.

Put beaten eggs in a bowl, add 2 fl oz of the cream and the carrot puree. Season to taste.

Butter 4 coquotte moulds and fill each with the carrot mixture.

Cover each with buttered foil, place in a bain marie and cook in the oven for about 25 minutes, or until set.

Meanwhile make the sauce.

Melt the butter in a frying pan, add the prawns, saving 8 for garnish. Flambe with the sherry, pour on the cream, bring gently to the boil and reduce a little if necessary.

Add the julienne strips and season with ground black pepper.

Turn out the carrot mousses onto individual plates, spoon the sauce round.

Top each mousse with 2 prawns and a sprig of parsley.

Idonea Crossley

Littleton Farmhouse
Airlie
Kirriemuir

SMOKED CHICKEN WITH TOMATO AND GINGER SAUCE
Serves 8-10

One smoked chicken boned 3-4 lbs (If smoked chicken is unavailable, ordinary chicken may be used instead.)
4 oz cheese (I used "St Andrews" from the Howgate Dairy)
2 slices bread (made into breadcrumbs)
Handful watercress leaves
Leaves from 2 sprigs of rosemary
2 oz toasted hazelnuts
One sheet of buttered bakewell paper

For the tomato and ginger sauce:
14 oz chopped tomatoes
zest and juice of a lime
garlic clove - crushed
2 teaspoons fresh ginger (finely chopped)
2 oz chopped chives
a dash of Tabasco
seasoning

1. Bone the smoked chicken or ask your butcher to do this for you.
2. Lay chicken on a large sheet of buttered bakewell paper and redistribute chicken flesh to cover skin equally.
3. Whizz hazelnuts and rosemary leaves in the Magimix.
4. Add cheese and breadcrumbs - whizz to bind.
5. Place in a bowl, add watercress leaves and season to taste.
6. Roll stuffing into a sausage and place down the centre of the chicken.
7. Roll chicken to cover the stuffing turning up the ends to cover stuffing completely.
8. Use the paper to cover the chicken.
9. Roll the chicken in silver foil and bake at 200°C for 1 1/2 hours until juices run clear. Allow to cool completely before slicing.

Tomato and Ginger Sauce:
1. Place everything apart from the chives and zest of lime in the Magimix and whizz.
2. Season to taste
3. Strain to remove tomato seeds (if desired)
4. Add zest of lime and chives.

Serve chicken on the sauce with a crisp green salad.

This dish can be adapted using different varieties of cheeses.

Fiona Bird
(who runs her own excellent catering
business from Littleton Farmhouse)

Fifi Scott's
SMOKED MACKERAL SUEDOISE
(Serves 4-6)

1/2 pt (280 mls) single cream
1 bay leaf
juice of 1 lemon
1 level tbls gelatine
sprig each of parsley & thyme
40g butter   40g flour
freshly ground pepper
230g smoked mackeral fillets
1 egg white stiffly whipped

Heat the cream, parsley, thyme and bay leaf to simmering point. Take off the heat and leave to infuse for 10 minutes, then strain. Melt butter, stir in flour. Once well mixed, gradually whisk in cream. Continue whisking until thick, smooth and bubbling. Take off heat. Make up the gelatine with 4 tbls hot water. Mash the mackeral until smooth, add the sauce, gelatine, lemon juice and peper. Finally fold in the eqq white.
Pour into a 1 pint container.
Leave to set for 3-4 hours in the refrigerator.